My Child, His Child

My Child, His Child

Spiritual Blessings for Mothers and Families from the Ten Commandments

Diane M. Poythress

RESOURCE *Publications* • Eugene, Oregon

MY CHILD, HIS CHILD
Spiritual Blessings for Mothers and Families from the Ten Commandments

Copyright © 2016 Diane M. Poythress. All rights reserved. Except for brief quotations in critical publications or reviews, no part of this book may be reproduced in any manner without prior written permission from the publisher. Write: Permissions, Wipf and Stock Publishers, 199 W. 8th Ave., Suite 3, Eugene, OR 97401.

Resource Publications
An Imprint of Wipf and Stock Publishers
199 W. 8th Ave., Suite 3
Eugene, OR 97401

www.wipfandstock.com

PAPERBACK ISBN: 978-1-5326-0050-0
HARDCOVER ISBN: 978-1-5326-0052-4
EBOOK ISBN: 978-1-5326-0051-7

Manufactured in the U.S.A. SEPTEMBER 28, 2016

Except where otherwise noted, Scripture quotations are from The Holy Bible, English Standard Version®, copyright © 2001 by Crossway Bibles, a publishing ministry of Good News Publishers. Used by permission. All rights reserved.

Scripture quotations marked NASB are taken from the New American Standard Bible® (NASB), Copyright © 1960, 1962, 1963, 1968, 1971, 1972, 1973, 1975, 1977, 1995 by The Lockman Foundation. Used by permission. www.Lockman.org.

Dedication

To my sons Ransom and Justin,
who so graciously allowed their lives to serve as a testimony to others.

They continue to teach me what it means to be God's child in relation to his Son Jesus Christ.

May the Lord keep them faithful all their days for his glory.

"There is therefore now no condemnation for those who are in Christ Jesus. For the law of the Spirit of life has set you free in Christ Jesus from the law of sin and death. For God has done what the law, weakened by the flesh, could not do. By sending his own Son in the likeness of sinful flesh and for sin, he condemned sin in the flesh, in order that the righteous requirement of the law might be fulfilled in us, who walk not according to the flesh but according to the Spirit."

—ROMANS 8:1-4

Contents

Introduction | ix

1. The First Commandment, Jesus Saves | 1
2. The Second Commandment, Jesus's Sacrifice | 10
3. The Third Commandment, Jesus Sanctifies | 19
4. The Fourth Commandment, Jesus Reconciles | 30
5. The Fifth Commandment, Jesus's Propitiation | 40
6. The Sixth Commandment, Jesus Justifies | 52
7. The Seventh Commandment, Jesus Redeems | 63
8. The Eighth Commandment, Jesus Adopts | 75
9. The Ninth Commandment, Jesus's Righteousness | 90
10. The Tenth Commandment, Jesus Reconciles | 105
11. Conclusion | 125

Bibliography | 133

Introduction

I SAT IN THE pew with tears running down my cheeks, embarrassed that the elder taking the offering saw me. After morning worship, he asked if everything were okay. I told him that my childhood friend whom I had known from the age of two was dying apart from Christ. My friend was the son of my parents' good friends, and we were born two days apart. We had gone on family picnics, hikes, played badminton in the backyard, yearly extolled each other's Christmas gifts (especially his train that puffed real smoke), visited each other when sick, been in the church choir, gone to the local amusement fair, counseled at church camp together, gone to a high school dance, and seen each other every week in church and Sunday school as long as I could remember. But in the intervening thirty years we had lost touch except for occasional updates through our parents. I knew that his high school prank of hiding alcohol in a hair tonic bottle in his gym locker had turned into an addiction.

My friend and I had never heard the gospel, even though we went to a conservative church. Our minister had used doublespeak to convince the pastoral search committee that he was orthodox. But he wasn't. He had charisma, youth, good looks, energy, affability, but not the gospel. We only heard about modern psychology each Sunday, loosely based on a verse of Scripture. None of the youth in that church were saved until after leaving for college, or for hippie communes, or for jobs. Now my friend only had a few days of life left. I prayed. I fasted. I phoned. By God's mercy, I got through to his hospital room even though he was in intensive care.

Introduction

"You know our pastor never told us the truth. We are sinners who need to believe in Christ. He died instead of us, taking our punishment. You need to believe in him, tell him your sins, and give him your life and ask him to come into your heart to make you new, to give you a new heart." I ran the words together, trying to squeeze in everything I could, knowing our time might be short. He seemed alert and coherent.

"You know, you sound just like this new minister from the church who has been visiting me at the hospital."

"Listen to him. He is telling you the truth. You have to repent and believe in Jesus in order to be saved. You know I did this several years ago. God will give you a whole new life."

"I don't have much time for any life."

"You have an eternity of life yet. Please, please give your heart to Jesus."

"The doctors are here. I've got to go."

"Okay, but I'll keep praying, and I'll call again."

I found out that an interim, retired pastor who knew the gospel was temporarily filling in at the church. Praise God! The man might not have known it, but he could have been sent just at that time for the express purpose of bringing salvation to my friend.

Salvation belongs to God. He alone accomplished it, owns it, and grants it. Jesus alone in all of history took our wickedness and was punished for it, instead of us. The Bible says, "There is salvation in no one else, for there is no other name under heaven given among men by which we must be saved" (Acts 4:12). And Jesus himself says, "I am the way, the truth, and the life. No one comes to the Father except through me" (John 14:6). Death could not hold him. In him alone is the source of eternal life.

I had said the same truths to my children. I had heard unbelief in their voices and seen it in their actions. As I sat one day with tears running down my cheeks again, deeply pained over the disappointment I experienced in my children, God brought to mind the lessons that are contained in this book. Yes, they had failed miserably in so many ways, but so had I. Just as I couldn't believe a child of mine would ever behave in that way or make such horrid

INTRODUCTION

choices, neither could God abide my behavior as a so-called child of his. My outrage cried out, "Not my child! My child would never act like that. This couldn't possibly be my child."

Similarly, my own thoughts and actions cried out, "I cannot be a child of God! Satan is right. I am nothing but a hypocritical fraud, full of dead men's bones." Then God's Spirit reminded me that although I had committed cosmic treason multiple times, the eternal Son of God had not. The Father could look at Jesus and say, "That is not something my child ever did, or ever will do. It was not my child who sinned." Because Jesus always obeyed, and always loved and glorified his Father perfectly, I had hope of being called "his child." If my life were hidden in Christ, then his goodness would be mine and my sin would have been his on the cross. God's plan for the great exchange would have been in place in eternity. If I were God's child in Christ, then he loved me before the foundation of the world. Nothing I did would ever make him love me more . . . or less. His love was and always would be perfect and full. My longing to be known by my God, my maker and purchaser, satisfied itself in his knowing me as his child forever.

My failing to believe God and the failings of my children are still very real. Several are recounted in this book. Some may find their curiosity piqued by the instances cited from the lives of our sons. I would hope that the anonymity I have granted them, by not mentioning which son did which thing, would be honored. They have both agreed to the publishing of these stories. They have been forgiven, as have I, by a gracious savior who is our refuge. Yet God in Scripture has used fallen men to warn us and instruct us (1 Cor 10:11; Heb 11). He used Peter's sins and Paul's repeated testimony of his own unregenerate rebellion. While I have laid bare my own heart, I pray that God, through the work of Christ's Spirit, would use these poor words to lay bare the thoughts and intentions of others. May hearts be reborn, cleansed, and sanctified for the praise of his glorious name.

In this book, not every one of the Ten Commandments is handled from every angle. This is not an exegesis of Exod 20. It is an attempt to show how we and our children are all sinners and how Jesus is a great savior. The format is simple: examine the Ten Commandments for how my child has broken them, how I have broken them, and how Jesus kept them. Each chapter also focuses on one way in which Jesus accomplished our salvation.

I am aware of the various arguments concerning the continuation of the law and its application to the different commandments. Quite simply, I have taken the view from Romans that the law is good (Rom 7:12) and cannot make me sin. But neither can it make me good or save me. It merely points to the problem of sin in the heart, but does not solve that problem. Therefore, it shows me my sin and the necessity of Jesus's work on my behalf. But now having died to sin, I can see how to love and please God by looking at the law. "And this is love that we should walk according to his commandments" (2 John 1:6). To love God with all our heart, mind, soul, and strength is the greatest commandment, and his law shows us how to do this. His Spirit enables us to do this by faith.

When it was Mother's Day, my father took my sister and me into the kitchen to make a breakfast tray. He showed us how to make the cinnamon toast and which little vase to use for the flowers that I had picked from the yard. He brought down the fancy glasses from the high shelf for us to fill and found a pretty napkin to add to the tray. Part of my delight in that preparation was in serving my mother something I thought was a surprise. But I now also realize that another part of the delight came from Daddy guiding us in what would make her happy. I trusted him to know which foods, which plates, arranged which way would bring a smile. I think the law and Spirit do the same for a Christian. They show us and guide us into serving our Father in a way that pleases him and brings him glory. The law actually reveals my Father's heart. So now I enjoy learning the law and thinking about it. I can understand how David loved the law, meditating on it as something sweet (Ps 19:10). That is the kind of heart attitude that comes through faith.

Without faith, we can do nothing and are condemned by our own impiety. With faith, we can do all things through Christ who

INTRODUCTION

strengthens us. We can join the witnesses in Heb 11, who by faith fought lions, the world, the flesh, and the devil. Faith comes as a gift from God, through hearing his word. All of our obedience or pleasing God depends on this. Without faith, our best good deeds are saturated in the vile sin of unbelief. With faith, our worst deeds are dipped clean in the bleach of Jesus's blood. "Therefore perfidy or unbelief is the true root of all other sins . . . therefore faith alone suffices for destroying all sins."[1] Faith is the key to love which is the fulfillment of the law.

Do you care about someone without faith who is separated from God? We all have known a lost loved one for whom we longed and prayed. Is there any greater pain than to watch them daily walk further into sin and death and hell? How our hearts yearn to embrace them, to tell them God will forgive them when they turn to him. "For the Lord your God is gracious and merciful and will not turn away his face from you, if you return to him" (2 Chron 30:9). We love them, yet cannot touch their innermost being. Nevertheless, God can. "I will remove the heart of stone from your flesh and give you a heart of flesh" (Ezek 36:26). God can make the dead rise to life physically, and spiritually.

Going back to the story of my friend with whom I had spoken on the phone, God saved my childhood playmate, giving him a few extra weeks to grow in his love for him. Now I will once again sing together with him in worship someday. He didn't have much time to practice making God first. Yet his heart had been reborn into a loving submission to the one God, greater than he. On the other hand, I had to continue living, daily learning to be God's child through his only begotten Child, daily growing in making God first because he made me and bought me, daily walking by faith through trials.

Are you a child of God, or are you not sure? Perhaps after reading some of the following chapters, you will want to revisit this question. Even righteous Job saw himself as vile (Job 11:4). Remember that Jesus came to save sinners, not "good" people. Jesus died in the place of sinners, because he loved them. He loved you

---

1. Johannes Oecolampadius, *In Isaiam Prophetum*, 211r.

INTRODUCTION

and me. Confess your sins. Tell him you are vile. Ask him to put those sins on the cross with Jesus. Believe Jesus took the punishment for them instead of you. Ask your Father to forgive you and wash you. Now rise up, accepted and purified through God's Son, and walk in newness of life. Now is the time, if the Spirit is calling you. Come to his table to feast on the fruits of Jesus's work now.

1

The First Commandment

Jesus Saves

> You shall have no other gods before me. (Exod 20:3)

LIKE MANY CHRISTIAN MOTHERS, I prayed that my children would be filled with the Holy Spirit even before they were born. Rocking them in my arms at night, I thought heaven had come to earth. Surely, this beautiful bundle, just freshly created, must know that God made him. His little heart certainly must bubble over with love for God his maker.

Then it happened. College dining halls are not the only place where food fights occur. I sat next to my son's highchair with a spoonful of baby food aimed at his mouth. "Open," I urged. Suddenly he sealed his lips and turned his head away. He understood the command and had defied it. I wept bitter tears knowing that sin had reared its ugly head and won. My beautiful baby was a sinner. "No, Lord, not my child. Let him always be faithful to you," I had sobbed. It was not the last of such prayers.

What does it mean to have no other god?

Sin, however, is not just a childish affliction, nor is it a mere outward act. A legend about C. H. Spurgeon relates how a man entered this pastor's office, bragging that he had no sin. Spurgeon got up from his seat, went around the desk, stomped on the man's foot, and said, "Now that we have taken care of that foolishness, let's talk." Sin is an attitude of rebellion against God, which may or may not be expressed toward man. God does not have first place in our heart. We care more about our own reputation, family, job security, or friendships. We have accumulated gods and multiplied them so as to shut out the real God. These substitute masters block us from pursuing the true God. "Any man of the house of Israel who sets up his idols in his heart, puts right before his face the stumbling block of his iniquity" (Ezek 14:4 NASB).

We might even rationalize that we are serving the true God by serving imitations. Our hearts are so wicked and deceitful. They refuse to recognize God as God. They are hopelessly corrupted. They must be made over. They must be made again, born again. Jesus said, "Unless one is born again, he cannot see the kingdom of God" (John 3:3).

So how could I help my son? I wanted desperately to reach into my child and fix his heart. I couldn't. Only God can make us and then remake us. Without God's exclusive decision to change my baby, he would continue in sin's growing, entwining power, becoming enslaved to his own evil will and ending up in hell and eternal death.

The very first of the Ten Commandments tells us. "I am the Lord your God who brought you out of the land of Egypt, out of the house of slavery. You shall have no other gods before me" (Exod 20:2–3). In Scripture, "Egypt" is often a metaphor for bondage, especially bondage to sin. Some might say they are not enslaved by anything, but Jesus said, "Everyone who commits sin is a slave to sin" (John 8:34). Since we have all sinned, we are all slaves. We all need freedom from our addiction to darkness. That does not necessarily mean that someone looking at us would see that we have obviously heinous faults. But as we go over each of the Ten Commandments, we will see through each of them that the basic problem is the same: sin is in the heart. We have all rebelled against God. It has happened at least once in attitude, if not in action. We are imprisoned. In actual fact, we are worse off than mere slaves to sin; we have been killed by sin. We are dead.

Dr. R. C. Sproul used to draw a picture on the blackboard of a man adrift in the water. "Is he yelling for someone to throw out a life preserver from a ship? No, he is dead." Then he erased the floating figure, drawing a new figure lying way below the wavy surface. "He is not adrift. He is lying on the bottom of the ocean floor—dead." What he clearly demonstrated in that drawing was that not only are we unwilling to acknowledge God as Creator and savior, but also we can't even want to be changed because we are dead.

Recently I heard someone say that a parishioner mentioned that he didn't really feel the weight of guilt for sin. His pastor replied, "No, nor would a corpse feel a ton of bricks piled on him."

We are dead in our trespasses and sins. We are deceived if we really think that we as dead people could choose to love God. One man, full of life, Adam, had no sin, no corruption of soul. He was created perfectly good. He had never known evil. He freely loved God, walking and communing with him daily in earthly bliss. But God warned him that if he sinned, then he would know what evil was, not only from the outside, but from the depths inside. When faced with a choice to either love God or rebel and become his own authoritative center, he rebelled. Now all his children, including us, have hearts bent the same way, before we are even born. We have rebellious, autonomous hearts even before we have the physical ability outside our mothers to express that rebellion. There is a dead soul, dead in its sin, inside a live body.

My child

This applied to my child as well. If only my child would embrace Jesus, then all would be well. I prayed intently, remembering God's promises, "For God so love the world that he gave his only Son, that whoever believes in him should not perish but have eternal life" (John 3:16). "Dear God, please remove his heart of stone and give him a fresh, living heart that believes in you," I pleaded. In God's time and by God's grace, both of our sons did confess faith in Christ at a young age, but that was not the end of their struggling to love God first in their lives, either for them or for me. I vividly remember one instance.

"What do you mean 'he's not there'?" I could hear my voice rising. "He should have gotten to your house over an hour ago. Where else could he be? "

Only silence came from the other end of the phone. Our son who was in a rebellious relation with us had told us where he was going. But he wasn't there. My husband took the car to drive the probable route. I began phoning friends where he might have stopped. Two other mothers offered to drive roads to see if they could find him. The teen boy next door began phoning friends. All to no avail. We phoned the church for prayer and then phoned the police. I sat down and cried and prayed. He might be dead somewhere. Even worse: he might be dead and not be saved, and then I would never see him again. My heart ached so badly that it felt like it had contracted into a spasmed ball inside of me. "Please, God, let him be alive. Give him time to repent."

Later I wondered, "Does God ever feel like this? Is this how God felt when Adam sinned, and hid so he could not be found?" What about when Israel was lost and he said, "My heart is turned over within me, all my compassions are kindled" (Hos 11:8). God had grieved deeply for his child.

As the policeman was leaving with a photo, description, and report, in walked the lost prodigal—two minutes before curfew. He smiled with a not-a-care-in-the-world look, as if nothing had happened. He had gone to another boy's home whom we didn't know, and he didn't think it would matter as long as he was back on time.

My attitude

I was so relieved. I cried some more. My heart loved that child more than it loved God. I would have fought God for that child's safety and salvation. It was right for me to want him safe and saved. It was not right for me to become adversarial to God, to complain against him. I was telling God that if he took my child at that point, his way was not right (Ezek 18:25). My son had replaced God as first in my heart. I had broken the covenant. God was not my God, and I was not his people, not his child.

It was years before I learned what Spurgeon knew. "Favourite children are often the cause of much sin in believers; the Lord is grieved when he sees us doting upon them above measure; they will live to be as great a curse to us as Absalom was to David, or they will be taken from us to leave our homes desolate. If Christians desire to grow thorns to stuff their sleepless pillows, let them dote upon their dear ones."[1]

My sons found other ways to dishonor and rebel, hurting me deeply. They often betrayed their upbringing and the love showered on them. But I had committed a far greater treason. We all have. We have committed cosmic treason. We have placed something or someone higher than God. For me, I had loved my children more than God. I broke the first commandment. "Can man make for himself gods? Such are not gods" (Jer 16:20).

A mother is sometimes called like Abraham to put her child on the altar, saying, "Not my will, but Thine be done." Have you had to relinquish your child to death? Maybe it is spiritual death rather than physical. Have you had to sacrifice your child due to geographic distance, prison, overindulgence in work, sickness, an alienating marriage, deep emotional scars? Any of these might come through your hand or the child's. The pain of such a sacrifice can twist the soul into a paralyzing agony.

---

1. Spurgeon, *Morning and Evening*, 250.

Other gods

But it is not always our children who occupy the pedestal of honor. Usually the daily competing gods come in a more mundane, less crucial form. Every day we must make decisions about what it is that we love the most. Do we love God above all else? Is there something that we love more that must be relinquished? Perhaps it is our own peace and quiet, our vocation, our status, or our vanity. Sometimes the competitor for God's love is not a what, but a who. In any case, God asks, "Do you love me more than anything else, more than these?"

Why does God demand this preeminence? Another scene flashed into memory. "Daddy, why should we give our hearts to Jesus?" Little Craigy had bounced into the kitchen, interrupting his father's lunch despite my babysitting efforts. As a new Christian, I held my breath, thinking what I would say to answer that question and to simplify all the complicated implications of scriptural doctrines for such a young child. With no hesitation, his father, R. C. Sproul, answered, "Because he made us and bought us."

Of course! All the ideas of God's creator transcendence and our finite creatureliness, all that God spoke concerning his will and love, sovereignty and mercy, all about his redemption due to our sinful corruption and his great salvation through the work of the cross, all of that contained in the few words: "He made us and he bought us." There is no other God. No one else is Creator and rescuer. Here is the foundation stone laid through Christ for all of faith and life. There is no other God. Only God is Creator. Only God is savior.

Christ

Jesus's very name, "God saves," demonstrated his mission. "He will save his people from their sins" (Matt 1:21). He alone was eligible since he alone in all of history was without sin. He kept the covenant perfectly. He was holy. God the Father was always his God first and foremost in every situation. He didn't even speak on his

The First Commandment

own, but only spoke the words that his Father gave him. He always glorified God, did his work, and manifested his name (John 17:4, 6). He always loved his Father above all else and had no other gods. He kept the covenant perfectly by being God's perfect reflection, God's perfect child. Because of that, Jesus could die as the savior, taking our sin, our due punishment of death. No one else could do this, since they already carried the death penalty for their own sins.

So he accomplished salvation from sin and death, and now possesses the fruit. He can give it to anyone he wants. He is the source of salvation. "And being made perfect, he became the source of eternal salvation to all who obey him" (Heb 5:9). Because of his work of saving us by taking the punishment we deserved on the cross, he also received authority to give eternal life (John 17:3). Salvation belongs to God and no one else.

Jesus submitted his own will and life entirely to his Father. When his body screamed for food, he rejected Satan's temptation to turn the stones to biscuits. When he needed sleep, he stayed up all night praying for God's guidance about choosing the disciples. When he encountered a murderous mob in Nazareth, he entrusted himself to God. When his friend Lazarus died, he refrained from rushing to the scene, for the sake of the glory of God. When he was offered the possession of all the world's riches, he responded, "Be gone Satan! For it is written, 'You shall worship the Lord your God and him only shall you serve'" (Matt 4:10).

In the Garden of Gethsemane, he pleaded with God that if salvation could possibly happen another way than through the infliction of hell on him, that God would do it. If God's heart turned over for wayward Israel, how much more for his beloved Son at that moment. The Father said, "No." The Son submitted, "Not my will, but yours be done." That is what obedience to the first commandment looks like. That is what he promises to enable us to do (John 17; 1 John 4).

Response

My children and I have to learn to make God foremost in our lives. It doesn't come naturally to a sinner, even a remade one. Only one person perfectly obeyed the first commandment—Jesus Christ. We need Jesus's model and instruction as revealed in the Scriptures, but mostly we need his resurrection power as actualized through the Holy Spirit. He can enable us to do as he did, to love God with all our heart.

Having no other gods is hard. Everything competes with him, including ourselves, our own egotistical being. Often I have cried and begged God. "Couldn't you continue your saving work in me and my child a different way?" "Must your plan include this tragedy in my child's life?" "Isn't there another way?" "Can't we just get through this without so much suffering?" I have not always (in fact, never) humbly submitted to God's will. My children have not always submitted. But God's unique Son did. Because of his making God first and buying me with his blood, I can hide in him, knowing that in the midst of painful sacrifices, those things that call for my love, God's love remains on me. Christ made the Father's will and glory preeminent. If I am in him, then Christ's perfect love of God is mine. I am saved from sin and death. I am loved with an everlasting love.

Big hurdles like giving up my children to difficult lives, or giving up my father and sister to death, giving up dreams of beauty, health, honor, or even perfect housekeeping, must slide into second place. They don't give up their honored place easily, and yet they must if God is first in my heart.

The new allegiance of my heart must be actualized in my life today. I need to ask God to help me recognize what competes for his love. I can confess that I can't love him with all my heart, soul, mind, and strength. I can beg God to enable me today to love my Father as Jesus did. I can repent when I fail and hide in Christ's promised righteousness.

But there is a seemingly endless array of little hurdles. I know it sounds so mundane, so trivial, but I don't want to remake the bed today. I don't want to clean up my part of Eden by taking off all the sheets from the bed, washing them, drying them, and stretching them back on. I am going to have to decide whether I will deny myself or serve myself. I know it doesn't seem momentous, yet underneath lies the demand of the first commandment. Who is God? Me or God?

Even worse is the fact that I would like someone to pat me on the back and praise me for remaking the bed. I want honor. I don't want to acknowledge that God had anything to do with it. Yet he made me. He bought me. Today, like every day, for you and me, the greatest challenge and privilege of faith will be to call God alone "Lord," and to be his true child by loving him above all else.

What can be done when God is not preeminent? If something holds first place, above God, we must repent and give it up to him. Our offering is not always voluntary. God sometimes takes it from us when we don't have the strength to give it up. I have had many occasions like the ones mentioned, where I had to give up my sons involuntarily. God the Father, by contrast, sacrificed his Son voluntarily. Out of his love for us, he gave all that he was.

2

The Second Commandment

Jesus's Sacrifice

> You shall not make for yourself a carved image, or any likeness of anything that is in heaven above, or that is in the earth beneath, or that is in the water under the earth. You shall not bow down to them or serve them, for I the Lord your God am a jealous God, visiting the iniquity of the fathers on the children to the third and the fourth generation of those who hate me, but showing steadfast love to thousands of those who love me and keep my commandments. (Exod 20:4–6)

My child

ONCE MY CHILDREN GIVE their hearts to Jesus, they will love him with all their strength all their days. Really? In what universe? If that has been the case with your child, then skip this chapter.

I can't even enumerate how many idols my sons made. There was the pencil collection. After repenting of this sin, breaking a couple pencils, and offering the rest to be given away, I thought greed for material goods was gone. Hah! Later came the music and movie collections, not to mention the action figures, games, and the book series in between.

Has anyone in your house ever idolized a person or perhaps an entire team? Sometimes you tell yourself, "It's good for him to like a team, to learn loyalty in good times and bad, to find models of discipline and even godliness among the players, to learn about strategy, sportsmanship, perseverance." Then comes the day when you walk into your child's bedroom to tidy up, only to find a broken pen with ink spattered all over the bedding after a disappointing team loss. Loving God with all his strength seems to have been redirected.

What is the meaning of an idol?

We live in a world of idols and idol worshipers (1 Cor 5:9–10). Step outside and look at the houses, cars, clothes, and toys that have garnered money and attention. Some are necessities, but not all. I heard of a pastor who once went to the home of a church member who had just bought a big boat. The pastor hung a large sign on the stern reading, "One unsent missionary." Materialism is obvious, but idols can also be subtle, sapping true love of God.

Idolatry is also false religious worship, mentioned repeatedly in the Bible. False worship doesn't require candles, crystals, or a lucky shirt. It's as simple as planning a meal instead of listening to the sermon while sitting in church. My heart is turned toward me and my needs in worship, and not toward God. "God is spirit, and those who worship him must worship in spirit and truth" (John 4:24). Like ancient Israel, I may come to church vainly. My body is there, but my heart isn't. God tells us as he told them, "Oh that there were one among you who would shut the doors, that you might not kindle fire on my altar in vain!" (Mal 1:10).

Masterful idols bind my heart and that of my child. According to the way God states the second of these Ten Commandments, in God's inscrutable plan, my polluted or purified worship of him affects ensuing generations, "to the third and fourth generation." We cringe when we read that Hezekiah didn't mind that his sons would be carried off to Babylon as eunuchs because he thought, "Why not, if there will be peace and security in my days?" (2 Kgs 20:19). And yet we sit comfortably, hugging idols that will damage even our great grandchildren.

My idols

God tells us that every sin enslaves us. "Jesus answered them, 'Truly, truly, I say to you, everyone who commits sin is a slave to sin'" (John 8:34). Idols seem to do it best. Their tentacles penetrate into our desires, our self-worth, our goals, permeating every aspect of our being. The most insidious ones are not material. As a pre-teen, I wanted to be Miss America. Everyone knew she was the most beautiful, intelligent, and talented girl in the whole country. If only I could be that, then I would bask in fame, envy, and adoration. So I would read the statistics about the weight and measurements of the last couple of winners and then try to exercise down or up into those Barbie-like numbers. Needless to say, it never happened. My sister became Miss Wheelchair Ohio and was runner up for Miss Wheelchair America, not me. I don't know that this idol died so much as I simply got too old for it to be feasible.

My child

These idols seem to offer a false momentary "saving." In actual fact, they facilitate our own attempt to save ourselves. My son wanted desperately to be first string on the team. Every day in the backyard he harried that ball into obedience through heat, rain, mud, and snow. When the posted team list appointed him to a second string bench seat again, his idol died. He could not make himself into the honored all-star, which would give him a special significance in front of his friends and the girls. The saving of himself by creating his own meaning as the adored athlete vanished. It would have been a self-achieved significance, a meaning that he himself created. God painfully turned him around to see his only value in his Creator and savior—at least until the next temptation for self glory. Jesus said, "If anyone would come after me, let him deny himself, and take up his cross daily and follow me" (Luke 9:23).

Some idols—beautiful music for example—reflect God in such a way that our heart may fasten on them as if they were God. Deceiving sin has taken what should have led us to God himself and substituted a counterfeit. We cheat ourselves. To quote C. S. Lewis, "If a transtemporal, transfinite good is our real destiny, then any other good on which our desire fixes must be in some degree fallacious, must bear at best only a symbolical relation to what will truly satisfy . . . These things—the beauty, the memory of our own past—are good images of what we really desire; but if they are mistaken for the thing itself they turn into dumb idols, breaking the hearts of their worshippers. For they are not the thing itself."[1] The actual autograph of God around us, which should prostrate us in adoration of him, is adored as if it were God himself. We create a forgery when we content ourselves with an idol. We miss the rapturous consummation of being our Father's child.

Idolatry is like gnawing on an imitation orange. Sure it is plastic, but it looks so real. I can feel the dimples and the slight give of the peel under my fingers. I can imagine the squirt of sweet-tart juice. In my mind, I can smell that citrus pungency. I can do all this while scraping off bits of plastic with my teeth. However, the true orange itself is what I need, what satisfies, what nourishes, what I long for. So it is that all idols prove less than what is desired, because our hearts desire God. Nevertheless, their allurement entices.

Other idols

After I was a mother, new opportunities for idolatry emerged. Even before my children were born, I was bathing them in prayers, petitioning God that this one might be the new Billy Graham evangelist or that one would preach with the powerful anointing of a Spurgeon. The kingdom of God would be established,

---

1. Lewis, *The Weight of Glory*, 4–5.

Satan cowered, hearts born again through these offspring. Worthy dreams, perhaps. But what happens when God says, "Not my plan. Not your child." The idol crashes. The dream dissipates like smoke. Can God's plans become my plans? At that point, my heart must believe my own words repeated so easily each Sunday, "Thy will be done."

There were other more mundane desires for me. I wanted a daughter to play dolls, dress up pretty, cook fancy foods together, have teas, do girlie things. I got boys who stamped on soap bubbles, ripped and dirtied every item of clothing, ate grocery bags of food at a sitting, and threw everything that came into their hands (whether it was a ball or not.) Another idol smashed. In his mercy, God very kindly gave me a good relationship with a friend's daughter. Because of her, I could on occasion wander down the "pink" aisles in the stores. But all my beloved dolls, doll house, and ballet outfits were eventually set aside. Did the idol die, or did I simply acquiesce to the inevitable?

I suppose I had just assumed that if we had a healthy child, it would be intelligent. Even my sister who was severely handicapped from birth with a form of muscular dystrophy had graduated from law school. Imagine the shock as I tried, patiently, every three months for five years to teach the alphabet to my son unsuccessfully. Even my husband, the epitome of optimism, who tried one day to teach him the difference between A and B, came away saying, "I could have taught a parrot by now." How many times did I rock that child in my arms, weeping and asking God what would become of him? The reality of another idol became evident. This, too, had to be laid on the altar of sacrifice. Eventually, we discovered our son was dyslexic. God led us to a doctor who helped him overcome his disability, so he was reading the adult Bible six months later. But the idol of wanting an academically superior child never had strength again. It had been broken in God's time and in his way forever.

Other different sacrifices of ideals have been offered by my friends in their own lives, which may be closer to your experience. One father taught music composition at a university but had

The Second Commandment

a deaf son. Not only could the son never be proficient in music, he could never hear or understand the notes his father wrote down in his symphonies. Another father who was himself an athlete, outstanding in football, golf, baseball, and hockey, had only two daughters, one of which was crippled. A childless Christian couple adopted two children; just months later, the husband died. Both children were morally and spiritually bankrupt, bringing only sorrow to their widowed mother. A college friend awaited with great anticipation the day of his marriage, only to return to the church a few months later to bury his wife and the new life inside her. A classmate longed to be ordained after returning from the mission field. Leukemia sapped his strength, leaving him only a few weeks of life after his becoming ordained. All these fought the good fight. I cannot say if any of these situations actually involved idols, but they certainly would have the potentiality of doing so for me. Each situation meant dying to a dream, a hope quietly cherished came crashing down.

Perhaps God has asked you to die to the idol of yourself in much simpler ways. You like quiet colors like navy blue, but your daughter chooses glow-in-the-dark green boots with purple flowers for church. Your best friend hands you a gift that someone else already bestowed. The phone rings in the middle of your meal preparation. Your name was not mentioned among those who volunteered for the church Vacation Bible School. Someone published a recipe that you thought you had invented years ago. Grandma has the TV news blasting again. No one noticed your new hairstyle. Why did that baby cry in my arms but not hers? My husband chose a quiet night at home when I wanted to get some fast food.

Each of these "irritations" represents a deeper idol of pride, vanity, or autonomous power. Each reveals a desire to serve myself as my chief idol. Elisabeth Elliot would have called such circumstances a chance to die, an opportunity to lay a sacrifice on the altar. The essential sacrifice is not the dream, the child, the achievement, or the relationship, but myself. "I appeal to you therefore, brothers, by the mercies of God, to present your bodies as a living sacrifice, holy and acceptable to God, which is your spiritual worship" (Rom 12:1).

What would have happened if people in the Bible refused to give up what was precious? What if Abraham had said, "You can't have my child for a sacrifice"? What if Esther had remonstrated, "Why should I risk my life for you?" Or if Daniel conceded, "It's no big deal to not pray for a month"? Or if Mary had said to the angel, "I'm not giving up my body, my reputation, or my chance for marriage"? What if God himself had said, "I'm not giving up my Son for such a wicked world"?

Christ

Christ chose to give up his life for us. He gave up having a family, having a home, having political power, having ecclesiastical power, having riches, having servants, traveling to exotic places, being liked by those in authority. He gave up comfort, his heavenly glory, heavenly bliss, being beautiful, zapping detractors with lightning bolts. He gave up life itself. He never had any idols. His Father was always all glorious. Nothing else shone with the sparkle of desire for him. Every temptation that we might encounter beckoned to him. Yet he was without sin (Heb 4:14–18).

Temptations were laid at his feet that we will never experience. We might have been tempted to grab that unwarranted first kiss. He could have bread at the drop of a word after not eating for forty days. If we just kept quiet about that apparent test discrepancy, we could keep our higher grade for college admission. Christ was offered all the kingdoms of the world, if he just bent a knee. I could go to the bar with my friends, then God might save them. Jesus could simply jump from the temple and convince all the Jews of his divinity, avoiding the cross.

His sacrifice of his sinless self consumed all our idols. My unfaithful embrace of every false god that crossed my path went up in the smoke of his offering. My many paltry, usually unwilling, sacrifices become glorious when hidden in his one final sacrifice. The idols have lost their power over us. Christ is triumphant. He willingly put himself and all that a man could dream about on the altar. The Bible says his Father was pleased with his sacrifice (Phil 2:8–11).

If I am in him, then I lay on that altar in him. My idol of myself was consumed as a living sacrifice "holy and acceptable to God, which is your spiritual worship" (Rom 12:1). Christ gave everything on the cross and his love encompassed me in that love there on that cross. His offering included me. Not that I could in any way be the sacrifice pleasing to God, but God wrapped me into his loving acceptance of his Son's offering.

Response

How do we even begin to toss out these ancient masterful enslavers? What would an iconoclastic day, a day of breaking idols, look like? Maybe, for me, it should start with a prayer just to recognize idols. This morning, my husband left to travel several states away on a train. I found myself leaving the computer more often, unfocused, wondering what he was doing and whether he made his connections. God was showing me that I was anxious, wanting the safety of my husband for my own sake and forfeiting the peace that comes from submitting to whatever God plans. I repented. Watering the flowers, I noticed one of my favorite blue ones was dying. Something inside me retracted as I looked at the drooping brown heads. I guess these flowers had become an idol, because I was ready to fight God's clear will for them. I repented. A phone call came with an invitation to a women's gathering. I tried to sound interested although I didn't want to go. I realized that I spent more thought about how to make myself sound congenial than really caring for the other person's concern as a hostess. I repented. Crash! There went another idol of pride, along with several other idols, and the day wasn't half over!

But the power of God is presently at work, shining a light in the dark niches where grubby demagogues live in my heart. Ugly things hidden in the recesses are being pulled out and tossed in the trash. Is there any end to the number of them? Calvin says our heart is like a factory constantly producing new idols. Jesus has come not only to show me what a manufactured idol looks like, but to shut down the factory. God has revealed who he is, and none of my false gods or false worship of the true God are acceptable to him.

How shall we resist? Our Father's persistent, faithful love toward us and in us cuts the binding ropes of now impotent idols. Those encompassing idols are daily losing their control. Why? Because of who God is and how he loves me through Christ's sacrifice. Now when my thoughts return to a snub from one of my children, although it still hurts, I remember that I am not defined by my children, but by God's love. Icons that gave me meaning apart from God, things that in a sense "saved" me, are shredded. My meaning in life is increasingly encompassed by his plans and his glory, not mine. Because God has set his love on me from all eternity, promised himself to me in all his fullness, and given me himself in his Spirit, I can drop the security blankets in order to embrace and be embraced by the king of the universe, my Father. It is a life long process to both identify and reject idols. Yet God calls us to trust in Christ's sacrificial offering of himself on the altar where all our idols were burned.

3
___

The Third Commandment

Jesus Sanctifies

> You shall not take the name of the Lord your God in vain, for the Lord will not hold him guiltless who takes his name in vain.

A FEW WEEKS INTO the school year, I took my turn carpooling students, all from Christian homes. Suddenly the backseat conversation was punctuated with "Oh, my G—!" I pulled over, knowing I had to deal with this publicly, since all the little ears had heard this. "Does anyone know what the third commandment says?" The rote answer came, "You shall not take the name of the Lord your God in vain." So I prodded, "What does that mean?" Silence. "It means that you don't use God's name unless you are talking to him or about him. I can look at all the wonderful trees and say, 'Oh, my God, you are wonderful and make such awesome things!' Or I can say, 'My God creates beauty everywhere.' But you can't just say, 'OMG' or 'Jesus' or 'Dear God' or things like that when you are not talking to him or about him. If you do, you are breaking the third commandment and misusing his name. Do you understand?" Mute nods from the seats showed they had heard even if they hadn't understood. I led them in a prayer for God to keep our mouths pure, before pulling out into traffic.

My child

"Mrs. Poythress?"

My stomach tightened as I recognized the school principal's voice on the phone. "Yes," I squeezed out as fear began to paralyze me.

"I was just speaking to your son. I want you to know that he spoke a profanity in class today. After interviewing him, I am assured that he didn't know what the word meant or what he was doing. I'm just calling to tell you, so you can follow up when he comes home."

I suddenly released my breath, relieved that it wasn't anywhere near the worst of my fears. It turned out, he had sounded out a new word on the bathroom door, a word that a classmate had challenged him to read. Coming back into the classroom, the classmate reported him to the teacher. He was promptly sent to the principal's office. My child's mouth, which had been fed Bible verses since birth, had chewed filth. "No, Lord, not my child! Must he be like the world? Must he be like me?" I cried.

Words

I was guilty at multiple levels myself, because the third commandment is not just a matter of saying God's name in the wrong context or using profanity. The third commandment includes vain words that subtract from God's perfection, that diminish his holy name. For example, when I complained, I was saying that God's plan for my life was not good, that he was not good, that he had not kept faith with me to be my God. My complaints joined the wilderness murmurings of Israel against God's good sovereignty. God said in Exod 11:8 that the Israelites in their grumbling had not contended with Moses, but in reality with him. Every time I complained, I was speaking rebellious lies against my heavenly Father. I was saying his way was wrong, and my way was right. My speech spattered mud on my Creator. Other people, including my children, sometimes heard my words. How many times did I cause others to question God's goodness, holiness, or perfection by my comments, complaints, or errors? How had I detracted from the divine majesty, grieving the Holy Spirit himself?

What does it mean to take God's name in vain?

This commandment encompasses not only taking God's name in vain, but abusing those who bear his name. He commands purity of mouth not only in how we refer to him, but also in how we refer to others, both believers and unbelievers. The Christian bears his name by bearing the new life of the Holy Spirit in Christ. The non-Christian bears his name by bearing his image. I could not disparage others. It was not just a matter of "If you can't say anything nice, don't say anything at all." I could not just refrain from cursing my neighbor; I had to actually bless him (Rom. 12:14). Each of the previously mentioned commands from Eph 4 and 5 is accompanied by an order to do good: ". . . instead let there be thanksgiving . . ." (Eph 5:4) and ". . . only [speak] such as is good for building up, as fits the occasion, that it may give grace to those who hear" (Eph 4:29). I have to love my neighbor and my enemy (Matt 5:44; 22:37). They are supposed to be blessed by my words. That includes my children.

My words

I wasn't born a Christian. In fact, I was twenty before I was born again by God's Holy Spirit. That meant I had all those years to pour out of my mouth everything and anything that brewed in my mind. For me, good speech was just a product of polite society. It was the expected behavior among adults. I had no idea what it meant to use God's name in vain, which I proved daily by my behavior. Like most people, I knew certain "four-letter" words were forbidden. But what about a rumor about that new student from overseas? An intelligent dirty joke? A communal groan about that teacher's droning on? An appropriate name for that guy whose car almost hit me, who should never have been given a driver's license in the first place? God's word says, "Let there be no filthiness nor foolish talk nor crude joking . . ." and "Let no corrupting talk come out of your mouths . . ." (Eph 5:4, 4:29). When I became a Christian, I had a lot of tongue scrubbing to do, and not just my own tongue. I had the responsibility of being God's appointed parental guard over my children's tongues.

A life begun in sin takes a lifetime to become holy. What comes out of a garbage truck is garbage. What comes out of a sinful heart is sin. What comes out of a born-again heart is life. My mouth speaks from the overflow of my heart (Matt 12:34–37). It is the heart that must be changed, not just some outward action formed by self-imposed rules for living. After becoming a child of God, I remember being shocked one day when I actually blushed over something that had been said. It was the first time I had had that reaction in several years. It confirmed to me that God's work of sanctification had begun.

Actions

This third commandment about not taking God's name in vain became even more weighty in my thinking when I realized that being a child of God meant I bear his name. Whenever I sin, God is profaned. Being called "Christian" means I am a Christ bearer. My life is hidden in Christ. Christ lives in me. Others see Christ through me. Therefore my life either elicits praise to God or blasphemous curses (Matt 5:16). Every time I sin, I break the third commandment. I misuse God's name. God has promised judgment to those who use his name in vain: "for the Lord will not hold him guiltless who takes his name in vain" (Exod 20:7). That includes what comes out of my life as well as what comes out of my mouth.

The Third Commandment

Our *actions* as Christ bearers can take God's name in vain just as much as our words. God told Moses that he would not enter Canaan. It was not because he dishonored God by what he said, but by what he did when he struck the rock. "You rebelled against my command to treat me as holy" (Num 27:14). At one point during the siege of Jerusalem the Israelites promised to free their servants. They released them, but then they took them back into servitude again. God says they took his name in vain. "But then you turned around and profaned my name when each of you took back his male and female slaves" (Jer 34:16).

When I married my husband, my name changed. Sometimes I wished my boys would have a different name than ours. The only slightly restrained edge in my voice reverberated through the house as I called my husband to the computer. "Did you see this photo someone took of our son? It's been tagged with his name for everyone to see what a fool he was!" I couldn't believe the shame that photo brought on my husband, on our family name. I could imagine my husband's students saying, "So this is how a seminary professor's child behaves. Maybe I don't need to listen so closely to his words." Then I realized that when I shame my heavenly Father, unbelievers might have the same reaction: "I guess if she acts that way, then I don't need to listen to his word." When I was born-again, my name changed. I was married to Christ and whatever I did or didn't do reflected on that name.

My actions

A local salesman delivered some food at our house. The children needed attention about a disagreement. I told the man to put the things on the table because my husband was not here. He made some comment that seemed to mean he thought I was implying my husband had died. I didn't correct him since I thought it would just be confusing to try to unravel meanings. Besides, he wouldn't be there long and the children required my intervention. A few months later he returned with another delivery. This time my husband was home. He asked how long we had been married. When my husband told him, he looked shocked and almost ran from the house. Then I remembered all the confusion and my allowing him to be misled. I had diminished God's light in me. I had used God's name in vain through my life. God's glory darkened before that man's eyes.

Even non-action, failure to act, can be disobedient. Every promise I make is an oath taken in the name of Christ, whether I say that formally or not. If I sign up on the church potluck list to bring a salad, and then negligently don't bring one, I break the third commandment. God says swearing falsely by his name profanes his name (Lev 19:12). Since I carry his name, when I don't do what I promise, I profane his name, I take his name in vain. I act as if I am not his child. An older woman once set an example for me by always saying she would do something, "Lord willing." At the time, I thought it was a bit odd, but I've come to appreciate the wisdom of her ways.

In one of those more rare moments, I actually witnessed the work of the Holy Spirit in my son, who risked a friendship by asking his guest not to use the Lord's name in vain in our home. He could have just passively ignored the remark. But he didn't. I thought about how we each needed the same bleaching of our souls—me, my son, my son's friend, the Bible saints. When Sarah laughed at God's promise, when Job cursed the day of his birth, when David as God's king sinned, when Zacharias did not believe the angel, the same purging needed to occur. God purified me and each of them in the same way as he did Isaiah. A burning coal taken from the fire on the altar touched their mouth and hearts as well as mine, just as it had touched Isaiah. "Behold, this has touched your lips; your guilt is taken away, and your sin atoned for" (Isa 6:7).

Thoughts

So my words and actions can honor or demean God, but so can my thinking. Maybe it was just a thought, introduced by a news article, or a textbook, or an overheard conversation. But suddenly a rebellious, scornful idea arises. The Bible counsels, "See to it that no one takes you captive by philosophy and empty deceit, according to human tradition, according to the elemental spirits of the world, and not according to Christ. For in him the whole fullness of deity dwells" (Col 2:8–9).

I can also take God's name in vain by passively not doing anything to protect his name. So much foul language and so many perverse visual images came over the TV, even in commercials, that I found myself in my mind repeating the world's words. I needed to do more than sign protest petitions—I needed to actively protect God's image in me. "Let no one deceive you with empty words, for because of these things the wrath of God comes upon the sons of disobedience" (Eph 5:6). I had to record only what was good and fast forward through the rest and set a filter on both my screen and my mind.

My thoughts

"Another earthquake," I thought. "Well, God said there would be many before he returned. Besides, I don't know anyone in that disaster area." Suddenly I was taken back by the realization that I didn't really care about those people or God's name among them.

Other, more insidious sins came from unexpected sources. As C. S. Lewis once pointed out, your greatest temptations don't come from a dark alley, but the smiling lips of a friend sitting across the table. When a girlfriend asked me to pray about a doubt she was having, I soon acquired the same doubt. How many others did I pass my doubts onto as well, even if just by way of confession or a prayer request? How many saw their faith waver because of my casting suspicion on God's holiness and thereby taking his name in vain?

The worst way to take God's name in vain, to deny his holiness, to deny him is to not believe. All men are created in his image, but not all have faith in him. When Adam and Eve did not believe God's word nor his person, they took his name in vain. They proclaimed the idea of a holy God to be meaningless. When men refused to repent at the preaching of Noah, they broke the third commandment by not believing God to be holy, almighty, and just. However, when Nineveh repented at the preaching of

Jonah, they honored his name by believing his word was true, that he would come and could wreak justice. Faith in the name of Jesus extols him and reflects true salvation. My faith is small. I quiver at the slightest rustle of a threatening leaf. Along with the poor father kneeling before Jesus I pray, "I believe; help my unbelief" (Mark 9:24). Believing him is the way to honor his name and not disabuse it. Oh, that God would give us grace to not take his name in vain, to hallow that name, even as we petition in the Lord's Prayer!

Christ

We can only do this through the sanctification of redemption. Christ was the stone that touched Isaiah's lips, that fiery rock, taken from the altar of sacrifice at the cross. Scripture says, "Our God is a consuming fire" (Heb 12:29). His white hot offering was applied to my heart in order to sear away my impurities. I am cleansed of my sin by his sacrifice. He has sprinkled me with the only existing stain remover—Christ's blood. My guilt for every idle word, my sin for every misuse of God's name in thought, word, or life is destroyed like a dry leaf in a bonfire. "How much more will the blood of Christ, who through the eternal Spirit, offered himself without blemish to God, purify our conscience from dead works to serve the living God" (Heb 9:14).

That offering of the Son daily washes and sanctifies you and me. "I will sprinkle clean water on you, and you will be clean; I will cleanse you from all your filthiness and from all your idols" (Ezek 36:25). Just as I wash dishes each day, God washes my heart each day. God has promised to complete this good work that he has begun in me (Phil 1:6, 1 Thess 5:24). Why? God's will is to sanctify us (1 Thess 4:3). The blasphemous life that scorned God and invited others to do the same is being renewed into the image of Christ. We are made alive to righteousness. Now others may see the good deeds that our Father is doing in us and through us, giving glory to him (1 Pet 2:12). By God's mercy, someone might someday even note enough resemblance in me to say, "There is a child of the Father."

The Third Commandment

Christ is the Father's only-begotten Son born for us, the Son who is given (Isa. 9:6), the one whose perfect reflection shows us the Father (John 10:30; 14:9). His life never disabused God in thought, word, or deed, but only magnified his glorious name (John 8:29; 12:49–50; 17:4). Through him God has exalted above all things his name and his word (Ps 138:2), so that his name might be hallowed on earth as it is in heaven. For Jesus is the name, the only name given on earth among men by which we can be saved (Acts 4:12). His is the name God promised to reveal to his people, which we would then proclaim (Isa 52:6–7). All who call on that name shall be saved (Acts 2:21). We shall have life in his name (John 20:31). And we who are baptized in his name shall bear his name triumphantly, doing all in the name of Jesus (Col 3:17). "The one who conquers, I will make him a pillar in the temple of my God. Never shall he go out of it, and I will write on him the name of my God, and the name of the city of my God, the new Jerusalem, which comes down from my God out of heaven, and my own new name" (Rev 3:12). For Christ has the name above all names (Phil 2:9), so that "at the name of Jesus every knee should bow, in heaven and on earth and under the earth, and every tongue confess that Jesus Christ is Lord, to the glory of God the Father" (Phil 2:10).

Response

God's Son lived and spoke only what honored his Father. He never took his name in vain by speaking corruptly. He never took his name in vain by acting corruptly. All of his thoughts centered on glorifying his Father. That perfect purity is now working in me through his Holy Spirit. Yes, I still hear crude and rude words that I want to repeat. I still have to ask my son, "Did you ever hear us use that word? If not, then don't you use it." I still spill unkind sentiments when the jar of my heart is bumped. But just like with food, I am developing a taste for what is good. God is giving discernment as to when to close my mouth, confess the thought, and replace the impetuous word with what is true, pure, lovely, commendable, excellent, or worthy of praise (Phil 4:8).

My Child, His Child

My friend wrote to me: "I don't understand your prayer request about getting along with your son. What's going on?" I wanted so much to just tell her blow by blow all the pummeling I had taken emotionally from him. But I had just been meditating on this commandment and the Holy Spirit wouldn't let me. I realized that my son's reputation and name would be disparaged. I would be joining Satan's forces by adding to his accusations, condemnation, and mockery of God's family, of God's name. One small victory in a lifetime of battles.

But I can't do this in my own strength. The sin of my old nature keeps erupting and spewing filth both against my brother whom I have seen as well as my God (1 John 4:20). Each of my thoughtless words appears in God's records: "I tell you, on the day of judgment people will give account for every careless word they speak, for by your words you will be justified, and by your words you will be condemned" (Matt 12:36–37). Like Isaiah, I must fall on my knees to cry out to God that I am a person with unclean lips (Isa 6:5). I have sinned—again.

Instead of taking God's name in vain, I know that I can now wake up blessing his name, singing his praises, testifying to his mercies that are new every morning and recounting his faithfulness each night (Ps 92:2). I'm not saying I do this every day, but I am being conformed into the image of Christ (2 Cor 3:18). That means progress in holiness, progress in loving God and my neighbor, progress in glorifying God. That is what is happening. My heart is becoming a fountain of living water springing up to eternal life and spilling into the thirsty lives around me (John 7:38). I can look into the eyes of the young cashier and truthfully testify of God's goodness. God has prayed for me and saved me, just as he did for Peter who denied the Lord and swore (Luke 22:32). God will do the same for you and me as believers. God in mercy has taken us from the mud and washed us. He is our God and we are his people. Why? Because he is Lord of the covenant he has made with us.

We cannot in ourselves keep from profaning God's name. But Christ covers us with the purity of himself, sending his Spirit to sanctify us. Through Jesus, God can glorify himself in me.

The Third Commandment

"Through him then let us continually offer up a sacrifice of praise to God, that is, the fruit of lips that acknowledge his name" (Heb 13:15). He will work his will through us because he has promised, and he is faithful. His name is emblazoned on our hearts with a fiery branding iron of love that cleanses us and makes us his forever. He is holy; therefore we are commanded to be holy. And I will be holy, and you as a believer will be holy in word, action, and heart thoughts, because of the Spirit's work in us to accomplish God's promise. "And I am sure of this, that he who began a good work in you will bring it to completion at the day of Jesus Christ" (Phil 1:6). God's name will be hallowed in us, and through us his power and plan will be displayed.

4

The Fourth Commandment

Jesus Reconciles

> Remember the Sabbath day, to keep it holy. Six days you shall labor and do all your work, but the seventh day is a Sabbath to the Lord your God. On it you shall not do any work, you, or your son, or your daughter, your male servant, or your female servant, or your livestock, or the sojourner who is within your gates. For in six days the Lord made heaven and earth, the sea, and all that is in them, and rested the seventh day. Therefore the Lord blessed the Sabbath day and made it holy. (Exod 20:8–11)

My child

"Do I have to? None of the other boys wear a tie. Why do we have to be different? They are Christians, too. Where does it say you have to wear a tie in order to go to church?" Did you think that clothing fights only came with girls? My husband and I had decided long ago that covering our bodies was commanded by Gen 3:21. It was a simple rule of thumb, or two fingers for girls. Everything was covered from two fingers below the collarbone to two fingers above the kneecap, minimum.

But I had grown up with only one handicapped sister. The whole boy thing was new. Clothing style being more of a cultural phenomenon complicated the options. We decided that whether people knew it or not, clothing often reflected a person's worldview, ethnicity, income, and attitude. Our particular concern this Sunday morning revolved around the attitude. "When you go to a wedding, why don't you wear jeans?" I asked. "Because it is a special occasion," came the easy answer. "Right, and you want to honor the bride and groom on that day by what you wear. Well, God is more special and deserves more honor, so put your tie on."

Not all our attempts to sanctify the Sabbath carried objections. One sleepy boy turned to his brother at Grandma's, saying, "It's your turn to make the bed." "No, it isn't, because it is Sunday. I don't have to do it until tomorrow." We didn't always know the effect on the boys of honoring the fourth commandment and whether it just seemed like a countercultural legalism. Then one day, after a sermon on this command, our sons fairly ran down the aisle to the pastor. "I know just what you mean about not working on Sunday. It is the one day I can wake up knowing I have no homework. It's so great! I love Sunday!" our son exclaimed. You could have knocked me over with a feather.

What does it mean to remember the Sabbath?

The pastor had confided to my husband that compared to all the commandments in this series of sermons, he had read maybe four times as many books on this subject. What made it so hard was that culture had played such a strong hand. Satan had almost entirely erased the idea of Sabbath. The blue laws, which had closed all the stores on the Sundays of our youth, had now been repealed. Stores now find they make their biggest sales that day. The morning and evening cycle of church worship patterned after Old Testament temple commands by God had almost disappeared. Only after many phone calls did we discover a few churches who admitted to having evening worship. Instead of fellowship meals as a church, or families taking food baskets to the poor, or visiting the sick together on Sundays, people ran home to sporting events provided by TV or their own child's team.

God said that keeping Sabbath meant taking hold of his covenant; that is, he would be our God and we would be his people. "Everyone who keeps the Sabbath and does not profane it, and holds fast my covenant—these I will bring to my holy mountain and make them joyful in my house of prayer." (Isa 56:6–7; also verses 2, 4–5) The day was a sign from God that he would sanctify us and be our God. "Moreover, I gave them my Sabbaths, as a sign between me and them, that they might know that I am the Lord who sanctifies them . . . I am the Lord your God; walk in my statutes, and be careful to obey my rules, and keep my Sabbaths holy that they may be a sign between me and you, that you may know that I am the Lord your God" (Ezek 20:12, 19–20). It was a sign of our preservation both now and eternally. God sanctified that day in creation, through his command, through example, through the resurrection and through Pentecost. He equated breaking the Sabbath with profaning him. "They have disregarded my Sabbaths, so that I am profaned among them" (Ezek 22:26).

My Sabbath

When I first became a Christian, I began reading the Bible for hours on Sunday, trying to become acquainted with more than the few verses I had heard as a child. This was a delightful interruption in the weekly, grueling university studies. To conquer the whole Bible in a year, every year, became a lifetime goal, set for me by my college Sunday school teacher, R. C. Sproul. Then I thought it might be more helpful, and even holy, to fast every Sunday, so I could discipline my flesh and concentrate on God.

I continued to do that until I had an office appointment with my seminary professor, Dr. Meredith Kline, peppering him with all my accumulated, written questions. Casually, I mentioned that I had been fasting on Sundays since I became a Christian and wondered what he thought was appropriate. First he seemed concerned, "That is the worst day of all days to choose to fast." Then his face beamed as he poured out the glories of the Sabbath. It was a day to demonstrate before the world what heaven would be like. It was a day of feasting and rejoicing in the presence of our Lord, just as we would continue to do through eternity. It was a taste of heaven on earth for God's children. Sunday was like standing on Mt. Pisgah with Moses and seeing the promised land of heaven. It was our day to be raised to new life from sin and death. I went away changed.

After marriage and children, there were so many interruptions to the former disciplines of life. We had gradually fallen into the same slighting of God's command as had the culture around us. A nod toward the morning worship service sufficed for the day. Then God convicted us jointly during a sermon while visiting another church. I still remember the story that the pastor had told about a man who managed a large car sales business in Scotland. When an American firm took over the chain of stores, it insisted on Sunday openings. The Scotsman, as wise as Daniel, asked to be given some time to be tested as to whether his sales would go up or down if he stayed closed on Sundays. A month later, he was selling more autos than any other dealer in the country. He was allowed to close on Sundays.

After that message, we were convicted. We needed to make some changes. Thankfully, the children were still very young, so we explained to them that we had repented of sinning against God, which meant there would be some changes in our Sunday schedule. We began seeking out evening worship as well as morning. We made a more concentrated effort to direct our conversations and activity toward growing together in the Lord.

Implications of Bible verses began to stand out along with their promises: Exod 20:11; Lev 26:2; Deut 5:12–15. I began to wonder how many pre-Sabbaths had Mrs. Moses and the other women cooked extra food? What if Nehemiah had not shut the gates of Jerusalem on the Sabbath? Would Israel have been spared judgment if they had kept the Sabbath (Neh 13:16–22; Jer 17:19–27;

Ezek 20:13, 21)? Had the Shunammite woman been in the habit of seeking God's word through Elisha on Sabbath days, even before the resurrection of her son (2 Kgs 4:23)? What a wondrous blessing would the women have missed on Easter, had they not obediently waited until after the Sabbath to do what some might have called a work of mercy (Matt 28:1–9).

If God had killed a man for gathering sticks on the Sabbath, what must he think of me (Num 15:32–36)? He had mercifully preserved my life, despite my flaunting of his will, and I hadn't even known it! I began asking others how they "keep the Sabbath day holy." One woman had a meal after church where no topic could be discussed except the word of God. Another family made the TV, computer, and other outside intrusions off limits. So many new questions began to arise. If neither our children nor our servants are to work, which presumably includes storekeepers, what about machines? God cared for everything, even land, insisting that it, too, should have its Sabbath rests (Lev 25 and 26). How do I not become legalistic and yet care for the recuperation of creation the way God does?

We decided that at the very minimum, the commandment meant positively to worship with God's people and negatively to not work or cause others to work. Yes, exceptions for acts of necessity and mercy had to be considered, but those really weren't part of our own vocational duties.

Our sons had to make decisions and stand before God as well. The later phone calls from distant colleges pained us sometimes. "You are going where on the Lord's Day? What about church service? You did what?" Was this my child—the one who delighted in Sunday family games, worship, nursing home services, homeless meals, youth group meetings? Okay, maybe he didn't delight in all that, but hadn't he learned that it was better to be "a doorkeeper in the house of my God than to dwell in the tents of wickedness" (Ps 84:10)? No, he hadn't. Nor had I.

Attitude

God ordained the Sabbath for man, for his rest, but not rest in his own pleasures—rather, rest in him. "If you turn back your foot from the Sabbath, from doing your pleasure on my holy day, and call the Sabbath a delight and the holy day of the Lord honorable; if you honor it, not going your own ways, or seeking your own pleasure, or talking idly; then you shall take delight in the Lord and I will make you ride on the heights of the earth; I will feed you with the heritage of Jacob . . ." (Isa 58:13–14). Did I really think of Sunday as a delight when I dragged myself out of a short sleep to dress myself, my toddler and my baby? Even now, do I anticipate with delight the fellowship with God and his people, the hearing of the word? Or has it become a duty, a habit, a necessity. "But you say, 'What a weariness this is,' and you snort at it, says the Lord of hosts . . . Shall I accept that from your hand?" (Mal 1:13). I have forfeited God's blessing in my stupor.

I had to ask: do I act like God's child? Maybe I outwardly conform to some expectations, but what about my heart? God reminded me of his disgust with lukewarm love (Rev 3:16: "And so, because you are lukewarm, and neither hot nor cold, I will spit you out of my mouth."). He reminded me of his condemnation of reverent actions not flowing from the heart (Isa 29:13: "Because this people draw near with their mouth and honor me with their lips, while their hearts are far from me . . ."). And he reminded me of my less than concentrated worship (Amos 8:5: "'When will the new moon be over that we may sell grain? And the Sabbath that we may offer wheat for sale . . .'"). Did I rest in the Lord on the Sabbath for his sake or mine?

True Sabbath

But true Sabbath rest involved more than what we told the boys about not having to make their beds or do homework on Sunday. What I (and they) should have stopped working at was not mere trivial labors, but sin. Jesus said this was a day to be unbound from

Satan (Luke 13:16). My rest should be quitting the labor of enslaving sins. Jesus was to be my rest, the Lord of the Sabbath, the one who commands refreshment, and rebirth, who rules my eternal rest, begun in the present in him (Matt. 12:8).

The worst labor that keeps me from true rest is unbelief. Heb 3:18–19 says, "And to whom did he swear that they would not enter his rest, but to those who were disobedient? So we see that they were unable to enter because of unbelief." Sin and the worst of all sins, faithlessness, keeps me from Sabbath rest.

When I go to heaven I will no longer have to battle the world and its corrupt practices, nor my own sins that daily tempt me to evil, nor the devil and his demons who ceaselessly accuse and plot against all God's children. I won't have to contend with the effects of sin that make all creation, including my poor dog, groan. Yes, even our pet suffered. I wept to watch my little Shetland sheepdog painfully endure a disintegrating pancreas. How wonderful it was at that time to have God's promise that in heaven there will be no more death or mourning for us.

That is why a Sabbath rest still remains. "So then, there remains a Sabbath rest for the people of God, for whoever has entered God's rest has also rested from his works as God did from his. Let us therefore strive to enter that rest, so that no one may fall by the same sort of disobedience"(Heb 4:9–11). We still have an eternity awaiting where labor bound by the curse and hearts bound by sin will flourish freely unbound in the meadows of Christ's perfection. Then the Lord of the Sabbath, who on the cross unshackled us from sin and Satan and death, will say, "Enter into your rest. Enter into me, all that I AM, all that I prepared for you. I am your eternal rest, even now, already begun" (Heb 4:9).

Christ

The Sabbath in its essence is not a particular day, but Christ. Christ is our Sabbath, the Lord of the Sabbath, the final rest that is only vaguely pictured by the crossing into the promised land and Canaan. The year of jubilee has come for ransomed sinners. We can return home, for the Sabbath of Sabbaths has been accomplished in Christ.

Spurgeon enthused, "Here, my best joys bear 'mortal' on their brow . . . but there, everything is immortal; the harp abides unrusted, the crown unwithered, the eye undimmed, the voice unfaltering, the heart unwavering, and the immortal being is wholly absorbed in infinite delight. Happy day! happy day! when mortality shall be swallowed up of life, and the Eternal Sabbath shall begin."[1]

Jesus knew all that and yet while I was still a sinner demonstrated his love for me by dying for me (Rom 5:8). He stopped the war. God accepted a peace offering gift of one life instead of another, Christ's life for me. John Lennon can sing about no more war, but he missed the reason for war: man's sinful heart. And he missed the greater spiritual war between God and man where a peace treaty had already been made, signed in the blood of Christ. Now all those who believe in Jesus, the peace child, can enter the rest of eternal peace with God. The heavenly Father is now my Father, reconciled to me. "Therefore having been justified by faith, we have peace with God through our Lord Jesus Christ" (Rom 5:1).

We have on our piano a print done by my college roommate's daughter. It is a study on the Hebrew word "shalom." Worked into it are the words "wholeness, health, completeness, peace, safety, and wellness." All of these explain the meaning of the greeting and blessing "shalom" still offered by Jews today. All of these are fulfilled in the Messiah according to Isaiah 53. Christ is our shalom. He is our reconciler with our Creator, our healer of sin sickness, our sanctifying completer, our refuge, our rest from the curse of sin and death. He is our shalom. He is our Sabbath forever.

How can this be? Christ made peace with God for us through his flesh. My war has ended. I had no possibility of rest when I was hostile to God. Daily I fought against him, his people, his testimony surrounding me in all nature, his ways, his words. Though I didn't realize it, I awoke each morning in battle gear with a hardened heart to shield me from Christ's influence. I couldn't care less about Sundays, Christ, or anything that didn't seem to advance my

---

1. Spurgeon, *Morning and Evening*, 36.

own intellectual, social, or monetary profit. Little did I know that God was angry with me as a sinner, and opposed my wickedness. I was engaged in a furious war that I had no hope of winning, but where Christ had already been victorious.

Response

"So do I have to go to sleep when you nap? Can we just play quietly in our room?" My sons' questions always brought me back to ground zero reality. The battle with sin was not over. How to honor the Sabbath and keep it holy remained.

What did Jesus do? He worshiped in the temple and synagogue, read and taught God's word, walked through fields eating the grain, rested, and healed the sick and handicapped (Luke 23:56). He lived without sin, never breaking the Sabbath, never dishonoring his Father in any way. He always did what was good on the Sabbath (Matt 12:12; Mark 3:14). He did everything perfectly that I should have done.

Some of that can be imitated by us today. A day of kingdom business could involve tithes, ministering to the poor, visiting the sick and the shut in, practicing hospitality toward strangers, fellow believers, or poor students, growing in God, lifting up prayers, partaking in sacraments, hearing preaching, singing to him, meditating on God, his word, and our duties, and teaching or edifying others in both larger and smaller groups. Are there other pragmatic possibilities for making the day special, for sanctifying it, or setting it apart?

One friend sang the Psalms of Ascent while driving to church or listened to a sermon. Sometimes we played Bible-themed games. I made a special Sunday bag for my toddlers with Bible books, Bible puzzles, and Bible coloring pictures only available to them on Sunday. Everyone tucked into bed early the night before, with Bibles and supplies laid at the door and clothes laid out for the next day. Sometimes I set bread to rise the night before, so in the morning we would awaken to the smell of hot bread, reminding us of Christ's provision. My husband and boys prepared breakfast and lunch as acts of mercy to give me a rest from my normal weekly work. Leftovers usually comprised dinner fare. Missionary stories and devotionals got read aloud. Later we listened to a favorite preacher via computer. We could freely take walks together since none of us had appointments or time schedules that day. It truly became a day to act out before the world what heaven is like: a day of re-creation, set free from worldly cares just like in heaven. These are just examples of possible responses.

What I want to communicate, though, is not so much the "how's" of the way in which a family could approach the Sabbath, but how the truths of Christ's victory are inherently exhibited in this day. He truly is our peace, our reconciliation, our rest. "Let us therefore strive to enter that rest, so that no one may fall by the same sort of disobedience" (Heb 4:11). "I was glad when they said to me, 'Let us go to the house of the Lord!' Our feet have been standing within your gates, O Jerusalem . . . For my brothers and companions' sake I will say, 'Peace be within you!' For the sake of the house of the Lord our God I will seek your good" (Ps 122:1–2, 8–9).

My own spirit seems so flat, but the Holy Spirit in me makes me want to call this day a delight and wants my children to do the same. He tells me through Scripture, "Call the Sabbath a delight and the holy day of the Lord honorable . . . then you shall take delight in the Lord and I will make you ride on the heights of the earth; I will feed you with the heritage of Jacob your father, for the mouth of the Lord has spoken" (Isa 58:13–14). I want that, don't you?

My son once asked, "Mommy, isn't honoring the Sabbath one of the Ten Commandments, right along with 'don't kill?' Why do people think it's wrong to kill, but it's okay to break this commandment?" I had no answer. I still have no answer. I only know that I could do a better job and that I am trying to rest in Christ, my peacemaker, my shalom, who did do a perfect job. So we cry out with my other Christian family members through the ages, "Will you not revive us again, that your people may rejoice in you?" (Ps 85:6). May that start with us as God's reconciled children, hidden in the white truce robe of Jesus the peacemaker child " (Matt 5:9, 1 Cor 11:25, Col 1:20).

5

The Fifth Commandment

Jesus's Propitiation

> Honor your father and your mother, that your days may be long in the land that the Lord your God is giving you. (Exod 20:12)

My child

HIS LITTLE DIAPERED BOTTOM waddled as he crawled off on his chubby knees toward the kitchen where the waxed floor still shone wet. "Come," I said with a finger pointed down at the rug in front of my feet. We had tried to simplify command vocabulary when the children were young in order to achieve clear communication. He knew quite well what "come" meant after weeks of guiding him along with the repeated word. In fact, he no longer needed guiding and could be counted on to heed the instruction. This time, his head turned around to look at me, waited for the repeated order, then with a giggle took off for the kitchen again.

My child, my beautiful sparkling-eyed baby whom I had lived with and loved before he was born, had sinned. Not just any sin, but a sin of rebellion against me, the one who had fed him in the night, prepared pure foods, carried him everywhere, changed his smelly diapers, washed his stained clothes, twirled him in dances of love, read big picture books to him, held him in aching arms as he slept, shielded his eyes from the sun, wrapped him against cool breezes, sang to him, fell asleep praying over him. No, this could not be my child. This baby, the delight of my life, could never be tainted with sin. Not my child.

Many years later, my husband and I and our teen stood inside the cold front door of our house, waiting for the early school bus. I had just instructed our son on something he shouldn't do when a folded fist with clenched jaw and glaring eyes accosted me. That was it. The door closed as my husband led our son back into the living room for a "talk." All three of us ended up fasting and praying together that day until repentance and forgiveness flowed.

Where did we go wrong? How had we failed? Clearly we were not always just in our judgments, nor fair in our disciplines. We had sinned against them, against others, against each other, and their watching eyes had seen it all. But we loved them, sometimes almost too much. Didn't they know that? A dog does not bite the hand that feeds it, and yet our sons had rebelled against us. Something shattered and broke inside me. I knew they were born with Adam's sin, with an animosity toward God, and yet the demonstration of their sin somehow still took me by surprise. Did that enmity have to involve us, the ones who had looked anxiously into their crib, the ones who had loved them intently every day? You can count yourself blessed if you have never seen that grown treasure's defiant stare saying, "I am an adult. Stay out of my life."

What does it mean to honor?

Whenever I ask my Sunday school students what it means to honor your parents, the reply is always immediate: "Obey." This seems straightforward. Disobedience is the clear sign of breaking this commandment. A friend once taught us when our children were babes that obedience meant immediate, complete, and willing action. So, in contrast, disobedience meant delayed, incomplete, and unwilling action. I have seen children who flat out told their parents, "No, forget it, jump in the lake, and cry me a river." That behavior, left undisciplined, leads to stubbornness, rebellion, self-will, and pride. Obedience to commands that don't ask us to sin must be accomplished immediately, completely, and willingly (Heb 13:17). Such insolent children are heedless of God's punishment. "They are . . . disobedient to parents . . . Though they know God's decree that those who practice such things deserve to die" (Rom 1:29–32).

God's children disobeyed him, too. Adam and Eve had only one Father who created them in perfection and loved them perfectly. They in effect spat in his face and told him that they knew better than he did. Jonah disobeyed God quite intentionally by running away from what he was told to do. Samson defiantly chose to be yoked to a Gentile. Saul disobeyed the command of the Lord to completely destroy all that belonged to the Amalekites. In each case, consequences ensued. Adam and Eve died inside and were evicted from Eden with a curse. Jonah fell into the depths of the sea, barely surviving inside a huge fish. Samson ended up single, blind, and enslaved. Saul had the kingdom removed from him.

Actions

In this last instance, we get the additional instruction from God, "To obey is better than sacrifice" (1 Sam 15:22). What does that mean in real life? Coming into the house for dinner is better than delaying by picking flowers for Mommy. A scarred and inked tattoo of a cross on your body does not please God who commands that you shall not mangle the body he made in this way (Lev 19:28). Obedience is better than sacrifice—even sacrifice supposedly for God's glory. God even condemns those who promise to give money to him rather than caring for their parent (Matt 15:4–6; 1 Tim. 5:4, 8). The anger of God burst out on Uzzah when he touched the forbidden ark. David even called the place "the breaking out against Uzzah" (2 Sam 6:8 ESV margin). Uzzah's motive seemed to

The Fifth Commandment

be the protection of the ark, which, perhaps according to his own thoughts, would have been a good thing. But he disobeyed God. God considers the sin of disobedience to be like witchcraft, and stubbornness to be like the sin of idolatry (1 Sam 15:23). Honoring through obedience is better than our own definition of honor.

Clearly children are to obey parents and their heavenly Father. But then the question always arises, "When do they stop being children?" Studying Scripture brought me to the conclusion that we are always children as long as our parents are alive. Eli was reprimanded for not disciplining his grown sons who were old enough to be married and have children. They had to be at least thirty in order to serve in the tabernacle (Num 4:3, 23; see also Mark 7:9-13; 1 Tim 5:3-8). My seminary professor, Dr. Nicole, once told me how a friend who was a pastor had an unruly daughter at a Christian college. She used to sneak out of the dorm window at night after curfew. Because of 1 Tim 3:4-5, which says overseers must manage and control their children, her father resigned his pastorate. God honored that man's submission and brought this daughter to repentance. During Jeremiah's time, Jonadab's descendants refused to break the commandment of their ancestor from two hundred years ago. This was not just a father or grandfather, but a parent from generations previously. What did God say? "Because you have obeyed the command of Jonadab your father and kept all his precepts, and done all that he commanded you, therefore thus says the Lord of hosts, the God of Israel: 'Jonadab the son of Rechab shall never lack a man to stand before me'" (Jer 35:18-19). God blesses those who obey their parents.

Rewards accompany obedience. Our sons knew God's promise that he would bless a child with long life if he obeyed his parents (Eph 6:1-3). Once at the dinner table, our son exclaimed to his white-haired grandparents, "You must have really honored your parents a lot!" We laughed, but it made me think about other passages. God promises that wisdom flows from obeying parents (Prov 23:22-26), and also long life and peace (Prov 3:1-2), and honors (Prov 1:8-9), and happy parents (Prov 23:22-25). In all of this, the greatest reward comes in knowing we have loved and pleased our heavenly Father. "Children obey your parents in everything, for this pleases the Lord" (Col 3:21).

On the other hand, those who disobey parents are punished. Jacob's sons who attacked people unaware and slept with a stepmother forfeited the right of the first-born. Eli's sons died. Samuel's greedy sons could not continue in the priesthood. David's son who worshiped idols, despite all he had been taught by his father according to Proverbs, was told that the majority of his kingdom would be removed and all his work fall into meaninglessness.

It would be hypocritical for me to point the finger at anyone else, though. I had despised the discipline of my parents and not turned to them for wisdom. I had ungratefully abandoned them for school, a boyfriend, a career, travel, social gatherings—anything that competed for my own selfish attention. How often had I mumbled under my breath when asked to perform some chore? How impatient I proved with their old-time ideas and lack of energy! Often I cringed when they phoned, thinking we had nothing in common to discuss. Now I wish I could sit for hours at their feet to hear their stories, their testimonies of God's work, their wisdom learned—but it is too late now. What a miserable child I have been. How often I must have disappointed them and broken their hearts, just like my children.

One memorable time I actually obeyed my parents for a change and received God's blessing in my own life. When I returned to seminary, I wanted to save the little money I had by living with a widow or disabled person. There were people in the area who would give you free room and board in exchange for taking care of them. I had just been caring for my wheelchair-bound sister for the last one and a half years and felt this would be a good option. When I discussed it with my father, he dissuaded me, saying that I should do my studies undistracted, even if it meant dropping out a year to earn money. I struggled before God in prayer, thinking my plan was much more practical. Finally I submitted, although I was over thirty years old. I secured a dorm room on campus. That dorm had a common dining room for men and women. My future husband lived in the men's dorm, so we were often at the same large round table for a meal. The conversations began, and continued into late conversations when the floor sweeper would have to ask us to lift our feet to clean under the table where we still sat. God blessed my obedience to my father's advice with a precious relationship that turned into a treasured marriage.

Thoughts

However, so far we have only addressed the outward face of honoring parents through obedience. We have not touched the more expansive sense of respecting them inwardly. God makes this aspect clear in Lev 19:3, "Every one of you shall revere his mother and his father." This touches the heart attitude. It is possible to outwardly obey, as in Confucian ethics, but inwardly despise and curse your parents. God says, "Whoever curses his father or his mother shall be put to death" (Exod 21:17). This attitude is companion to defiance, stubbornness, unteachableness, self-will, self-righteousness, pride, judging, disdain, scorn, mockery, slander, and contentiousness. And it's not just a matter of "don't dishonor them," but God teaches us that we must love, and love effusively as he has loved us. "Love one another with brotherly affection. Outdo one another in showing honor" (Rom 12:10).

Some parents may not seem deserving of honor or respect, but God says we must love even our enemies. That kind of love is defined in 1 Cor 13. That love includes keeping no record of wrongs. I know a lady whose mother abandoned her as a child in order to live a selfish, wild life. That lady now has cared fifteen years for that aged mother. She has not kept a record of wrongs, but has laid down her life as Christ did for her. God himself is the ultimate definition of love. "But God shows his love for us in that while we were still sinners Christ died for us" (Rom 5:8). To love another dishonorable sinner takes godliness. It is always easier to see the splinter in someone else's eye, including our parents, than the log in our own. But love covers a multitude of sins (Luke 6:41; Col 3:14). Besides, we have all lost our honor. Only Christ can redeem that honor for us through his own perfect obedience.

My child

One warm summer's evening my husband and I went out on a date. We left the boys with a babysitter and several direct instructions countering previous problems that sitters had mentioned. When we returned, we discovered that we had not covered all the bases. The boys had run an electrical cord from our bedroom down the hall to their bedroom and set up a fan pointed at their bed on top of a wobbly pile of books on top of a chair. I don't know why we never thought of telling them not to do that one! They hadn't disobeyed any direct order and yet neither had they respected us by asking permission for such an undertaking. We began to use a picture analogy: reaching beyond the limits of your parents' directions and saying that you are still not directly disobedient is like having a safe, fenced in play area. Jumping over the barrier while keeping one hand on the fence is not safe. I wondered how they were stretching the limits at school as well.

Others

Honoring parents implies honor in other arenas of life. God specifies implications of this commandment for how we are to treat everyone else, especially those in authority. This includes grandparents, spouses, church elders, teachers, and governors. Not only should we respect our parents, but also all who are elderly: "You shall stand up before the gray head and honor the face of an old man: and you shall fear your God" (Lev 19:32). Husbands are to love their wives and wives are to "submit to your own husbands, as to the Lord" (Eph 5:22). We are to honor those who are overseers of our souls in the Church. "Let the elders who rule well be considered worthy of double honor, especially those who labor in preaching and teaching" (1 Tim 5:17, see also Heb 13:17). Everyone in authority has been put over us by God's design, and so we are to respect them. "Let every person be subject to the governing authorities . . . Therefore whoever resists the authorities resists what God has appointed, and those who resist will incur judgment" (Rom 13:1-2). Employers and employees, rich and poor, young and old, all have authorities over them (Eph 6:5-9). God expounds this premise in Deut 16:18—18:22, where judges, kings, priests and prophets appear.

My attitude

Not only had I dishonored my parents, I had mocked authority in general, authorities God had placed over me. By the way, did you hear the one about the presidential candidate who walked into a bar? Okay, I know, here I go again! How else did I do it? If I didn't think anyone was coming through the stoplight at midnight, I turned right despite the "No Turn on Red" sign. If the bathroom sign said, "For Handicapped Only," I excused myself by thinking, "I'll only be a minute." When the teacher ordered no talking, I thought whispering could be allowed. My husband might have wanted a receipt found today, but I put it off until tomorrow. God might command me to do all things without complaining, but surely he didn't mean all the time.

I had become my own little god, determining whether to honor an authority or not according to my own rationale. Following God's laws surely doesn't mean having to obey him without my own thoughtful interjections, does it? "If you love me, you will keep my commandments" (John 14:15). He never amends, ". . . according to your own time and situation and thought." Jesus says, "Whoever believes in the Son has eternal life; whoever does not obey the Son, shall not see life, but the wrath of God remains on him" (John 3:36). God is my supreme Father. If I am to obey and reverence my earthly father, how much more my heavenly one? "A son honors his father, and a servant his master. If then I am a father, where is my honor? And if I am a master, where is my fear?" (Mal 1:6). My most zealous, intense love for my parents should look like hate compared with my love for God, my savior (Matt 10:37; Luke 14:26).

How often had I scorned God's commandment to honor parents, authorities, and particularly my Lord, in favor of following my evaluations, my autonomy. I have been a miserable child of my Father, just like my children. Just like all people, I have turned away from his commandments, his person. Despite all the love he has showered on me in giving me the ability to walk and see, to speak and hear; all the times he fed, warmed, healed, clothed, protected, and comforted me. Nevertheless, I have run from him. Truly he can charge me with unfaithfulness and desertion. He maintains every right to fling me from his presence forever. His fiery wrath toward Israel in the wilderness should justly scorch me as well.

Our hearts

Ultimately, though, my sin reflects my heart. I act in unbelief. The work God requires, the commandment he wants us primarily to obey, is to believe Christ. "This is the work of God that you believe in him whom he sent" (John 6:29). In every respect, I have neither believed nor trusted nor obeyed the one who made me. God's anger should strike me like a flash of lightning.

So many people in the Bible received that ultimate condemnation, as in the time of Noah, or Sodom, or Pharaoh. God's own children also knew his displeasure as when David's baby died, or Uzziah became a leper, or Moses was barred from the promised land. The Bible says God was angry with Solomon because he turned away from following the Lord (1 Kgs 11:9). We feel sorry for them because we are like them. Deep in our hearts, we know that we deserve God's anger, too. It is just like when I was a child and made a face at my mother behind her back, but then she turned quickly and caught me. I flinched, knowing what I deserved. "God is angry with the wicked every day," and that includes me (Ps 7:11 KJV).

Christ

Eventually, the storm of righteousness did come, bringing God's just wrath. It did strike—but not me. Jesus stood between me and my righteous Father. The lightning bolt of judgment struck him instead of me. "We all once lived in the passions of our flesh, carrying out the desires of the body and mind, and were by nature children of wrath, like the rest of mankind" (Eph 2:3). But Christ, the true child, the perfect Son of God, took the full force of God's fury. He was "stricken, smitten by God and afflicted. But he was wounded for our transgressions; he was crushed for our iniquities; upon him was the chastisement that brought us peace" (Isa 53:4–5).

Jesus perfectly loved and obeyed his earthly parents, humbly submitting to them (Luke 2:51). He cared for his mother in her old age (John 19:26–27). He perfectly respected authorities as when he paid the tax and stood before the high priest, the king and the Roman prelate. But most of all, Jesus loved his Father with all his heart, mind, soul, and strength, never dishonoring or disobeying him. He glorified God's name in every movement, every breath, and every unspoken thought. "I have glorified you on earth, having accomplished the work that you gave me to do" (John 17:4). As Elisabeth Elliot says, "Jesus loved the will of His Father. He embraced the limitations, the necessities, the conditions, the very chains of His humanity as He walked and worked here on earth, fulfilling moment by moment His divine commission and the stern demands of His incarnation. Never was there a word or even a look of complaint."[1]

He believed his Father and trusted him in every circumstance and every twist of life, even through his cruel death. "Yet it was the will of the Lord to crush him; he has put him to grief" (Isa 53:10). For our sake, Jesus "humbled himself by becoming obedient to the point of death, even death on a cross" (Phil 3:8). God's anger spent itself on the beloved Son, not me, the treasonous rebel. "He is the propitiation for our sins" (1 John 2:2). God's just anger struck my substitute, his child, his only precious Son. This is the meaning of "propitiation."

Instead, undeservedly, my Father's unaccountable mercy fell on me. "Since, therefore, we have now been justified by his blood, much more shall we be saved by him from the wrath of God"

---

1. Elliot, "4 Elisabeth Elliot Quotes." See also Elliot, *The Liberty of Obedience*; and Elliot, *Discipline*.

(Rom 5:9). His blood doused the angry bonfire prepared for me. Now I am accepted in the beloved (Eph 1:6). "Those who were not my people I will call 'my people,' and her who was not beloved I will call 'beloved.' And in the very place where it was said to them, 'You are not my people,' there they will be called 'sons of the living God'" (Rom 9:25–26). Just as God instructed Hosea to retrieve unfaithful Gomer, he sent his Holy Spirit to retrieve me. Because of Christ, my heavenly Father opens his arms to me daily now, saying, "Come." "For his anger is but for a moment, and his favor is for a lifetime" (Ps 30:5). My inner longing for the myth of embracing acceptance by the perfect father found in fairy tales, or the prodigal son, suddenly becomes reality. This is not the "reality" of imagination. "But this story has entered History and the primary world; the desire and aspiration of sub-creation has been raised to the fulfillment of Creation."[2] My father (in the back seat of whose car I fell asleep as a child, trusting I would be brought home) was a picture of my all-powerful, all loving original Father, my real Father.

Response

I'm not sure that I am so thankful for my own aging, which the Bible denotes as God's mercy in my life. Perhaps some of my white hair has come from my own sons, as my relationship with my children shriveled every time they shoved me away. I just happened to hear by way of a friend that my son was traveling a thousand miles to visit someone else next month. Sometimes you think a knife in the back would hurt less. I jokingly commented, "If children are our reward, then I must have been really bad." Yes, I was. But having been accepted in the beloved only Son, God is giving me grace to forgive as I have been forgiven.

Today God is asking me to love and honor him because he is my original parent. I have already failed. When I met a recently divorced friend, I sympathized with her without pointing her to

---

2. J.R.R. Tolkien, "On Fairy Stories."

Christ's comfort. I tried to "make up for it" later by praising God's salvific work in my life to someone else. But what can I ever do to make up for snubbing the eternally holy God of the universe? So I go back to my knees to ask for forgiveness and in faith to believe he has loved me as his child with an everlasting love. I run to my Father to wipe away the dirt and tears, and to hold me in his everlasting arms.

We all fail in honoring parents, authorities and especially God himself. Ironically, we usually succeed best in honoring ourselves. It is not always easy to decide if we are doing something for God's glory or for our own. For example, I recently found myself almost competing with someone in telling stories about God's saving work. Sin has permeated even our testimony, every part of our being. But we can know God's word, so we know how best to love him through honor expressed in action and attitude. We can repent of dishonoring him and others. And we can trust that Jesus suffered the rod of God's condemning wrath. We can believe Rom 8:37, "No, in all these things we are more than conquerors through him who loved us." Then we can start again tomorrow.

6

The Sixth Commandment

Jesus Justifies

> You shall not murder. (Exod 20:13)

My child

AS WE CAME HOME, the babysitter met us at the door with a forced smile. It didn't take long before she narrated our son's escapade. He had instructed her to sit down and close her eyes for a surprise. When she opened her eyes, he stood before her brandishing his new pocket knife like a modern day Robin Hood. I don't know that we saw her or that pocketknife in our home for many years afterward. I had thought those situations only happened in comic movies. Surely that didn't happen in real life! That's something you would see in a Dennis the Menace cartoon. That could never happen in my family, not with my child.

Children have very little fear of death or understanding of its implications. Therefore, they often act recklessly. From this sinful attitude comes bullying, kicking, biting, hitting, cruelty, revenge, bitterness, hatred, insensitivity, lack of compassion, and unloving behavior. Children must be taught how to protect and prosper the gift of life, even in themselves. We decided when our boys were toddlers that all children were determined to kill themselves before the age of five. Both of our boys unintentionally pulled over bookcases on top of themselves when they were two years old; one fell out of a tree house, one swallowed a plastic coin, one pushed the other off the couch so that he cut open his forehead on a pointed coffee table knob, one took his tricycle to the top of the slide and got stopped by the babysitter just before careening down.

We are each careless with our own lives, even as adults. Maybe we smoke, eat too much or too little or eat the wrong things, try daredevil escapades, push ourselves to work without sleep, or experiment with muscle and energy boosters. We try to bend God's rules, hoping for no consequences. We bend civil rules, too. Maybe we drive a car in the slippery rain or snow as if the streets were dry.

My uncle took his son into the sheriff's office, slammed down the car keys and driver's license on the desk, and fumed, "These are my boy's. I'll be back to get them sometime. In the meantime, if you see him out on the road, arrest him."

Driving so as to recklessly endanger life was his crime, one that is common to most of us on occasion. Getting a driver's license means (as my son observed when he could drive) that you have a license to kill. A car carries the potential of death that no previous school supply bag did. I remember how much more carefully I drove after having children and how angry I became with those whose driving threatened to harm my little bear cubs.

What does it mean to murder?

Our actions reflect not only our uncaring attitude about our life and the lives of others but also flaunt God's reverence for life. Two major acts of God give our lives meaning, no matter what our quality of life or our circumstance. First, he made us, created us in his own image. "So God created man in his own image, in the image of God he created him; male and female he created them" (Gen 1:27). That includes everyone, no matter their physical flaws, including my precious little handicapped sister. He then allowed us to imitate him by creating life as well. "And God blessed them. And God said to them, 'Be fruitful and multiply and fill the earth'" (Gen 1:28). and Adam "fathered a son in his own likeness, after his image" (Gen 5:3). We are all God's mirrors.

Because all men everywhere at all times are made in the likeness of God, to kill a man means you remove the image of God. It is an attack on God himself. That is why God instructed Noah, who fathered the ensuing human race, "Whosoever sheds the blood of man, by man shall his blood be shed, for God made man in his own image" (Gen 9:6). Killing removes a created image of God, an image that God himself created. That is also why abortion, suicide, and euthanasia are forbidden by this sixth commandment.

God hates murder. In our car, we used to sing along with our sons to a CD based on Prov 6:16: there are six things, even seven things the Lord hates " . . . hands that shed innocent blood." Cain was the first murderer. He killed his own brother. Simeon and Levi took justice into their own hands and murdered a whole city of men. Joseph's brothers plotted to kill him. Moses murdered an Egyptian. Absalom killed Amnon and tried to destroy his father. Prophets were killed by religious leaders. God accused David of a murder that David had arranged, but didn't put his own hand to. Even Paul threw in his approval of Stephen's death and therefore participated in murder.

The Son of God was unjustly slandered, falsely accused, condemned, and murdered by men made in the image of God. We all put our hands to that death. There, at that crime scene, we all stood condemned as murdering criminals. "All we like sheep have gone astray; we have turned every one to his own way; and the Lord has laid on him the iniquity of us all" (Isa 53:6). If no one else had ever lived, my own sins would have brought the death sentence to Jesus my savior substitute. What greater charge could have ever been put to me? We are all murderers because we have all sinned, and our sin killed our savior.

God clarifies for us that murders and every type of killing are not the same. War by his command is not prohibited (Deut

The Sixth Commandment

20:16-18). Capital punishment as mentioned to Noah is commanded (Gen 9:6; see also Exod 21:12-17; Lev 20: 1-16; Deut 21:18-21; 22:20-24). Special allowances for accidents with no premeditated intent are excused (Deut 19:4-6). Animals may be eaten (Gen 9:3). Killing in self-defense is permitted (Exod 22:2). These fall into the category of killing, but not necessarily murder. Murder is an overflow of hatred in the heart.

Words

That internal hatred usually squirts out in verbal barrages. God knows these words are the tip of the iceberg of our cold hearts. At some point, the legalist will protest that he has kept the law and never killed anyone. But God's definition strikes deeper into the soul. "You have heard that it was said to those of old, 'You shall not murder; and whoever murders will be liable to judgment.' But I say to you that everyone who is angry with his brother will be liable to judgment; whoever insults his brother will be liable to the council; and whoever says, 'You fool!' will be liable to the hell of fire" (Matt 5:21-22). Hateful anger is just the unseen embryo of murder, which bears different visages once born. We can murder someone by verbally or inwardly mocking them, or by destroying their reputation with gossip, whether slanderous or truthful. In killing someone's reputation, we diminish their life. Every time we threaten someone with words or with a look, every time we curse someone verbally, or despise them in our heart, we have wished to diminish a life. The Bible says, "The venom of asps is under their lips. Their mouth is full of curses and bitterness. Their feet are swift to shed blood" (Rom 3:13-15). Harsh words and murder are tied together. I know that I stand guilty.

My words

There was a woman on campus who fit the Proverbs pig with a gold ring (Prov 11:22). She was constantly manipulating and flirting with men, although she was married. The men heedlessly welcomed her attentions, spending long hours talking to her privately. I warned my husband who then rebuffed her. But I found another woman to pray with and with whom I could let off steam. That became a form of gossip that I later regretted.

Words that bite can maim a soul throughout life. Criticisms can wound, leaving prominent scars. Idle words can pain interminably and break close relationships. I will never forget telling my college roommate that our other roommate had seemingly betrayed our friendship. Only later did I find out that this other roommate stood at the top of the stairs overhearing my sour complaint. An idle word spoken in supposed privacy had pierced her heart.

Thoughts

We can also be passively murderous by not talking to people, by deserting them, by abandoning our relationship with them. Isn't this the easier way out, rather than removing the thorn that is causing the offense? A young girl in my life for whom I prayed regularly, taxied places, remembered on holidays, mailed care packages to, and wrote to has ceased to communicate. Perhaps I sinned against her. But I will never know, will never have the chance to repent, will never be reconciled. Silence can hurt people; so can superficial interaction that holds you at arm's length saying, "I don't trust you to be part of my life, and I don't really care about your life." Paul passively approved of Stephen's martyrdom, which he later registered to his own account as murder. Onan's lack of positive action wasted the life of a child. God killed him (Gen 38:9–10).

There are many ways for us to commit murder, as the mystery writers and TV dramas demonstrate to us. But God defines murder as more than the ceasing of a heartbeat. No, we might not encourage someone to have an abortion, nor actually take a life by our own hand. However, we might wish someone harm, and that is what God includes in this command as well. Even a passive, unseen hatred of someone makes us a criminal in God's court. "Everyone who hates his brother is a murderer, and you know that no murderer has eternal life abiding in him" (1 John 3:15). Murder is not buried so far in our depths as we would like to believe.

My thoughts

One day I had a surprising experience of my own irreverence for life. Bringing the popcorn out to the TV where my husband had the game on, I overheard the announcer say that someone was injured. I asked my husband who it was. When he told me, I was relieved that it was not someone on "our" team. Suddenly a shock ran through me. How wicked of me! I determined that from then on I would begin praying for all the players both before and during the games.

It brought to mind the time our sons played Little League baseball. A child on our son's team had been injured, which allowed the other team a score. The parents next to me cheered. In shock, I had asked why they were cheering. The woman smiled, "Because we got a score." Then I looked at her in disbelief and asked, "At the expense of a child?!" She didn't get it.

An author in a book once asked a haunting question. What is your first reaction when you hear of a disaster in another city? 1) Do you go through your family and friend list to remember if anyone you know might be involved and then relax if no one comes to mind? 2) If it is a predominantly pagan city/nation, do you think "good, they deserved it"? 3) Do you think to yourself that you are glad it wasn't you and your town? 4) Do you wish such tragedies didn't intrude on your peaceful evening? 5) Do you begin praying and looking for ways to help?

Sometimes our wicked heart deceives us into thinking that bad is good. We might hide ugly aggression under the pretty umbrella of justice. "He had it coming to him," we gloat. The vengeance might be perpetrated by either our design or that of others, but the heart attitude is the same. God severely reprimanded the Edomites for both their attitude and their action. "For thus says the Lord God: Because you have clapped your hands and stamped your feet and rejoiced with all the malice within your soul against the land of Israel, therefore, behold, I have stretched out my hand against you"(Ezek 25:6-7). "Because Edom acted revengefully . . . I will stretch out my hand against Edom and cut off from it man and beast" (Ezek 25:12-13). God does not want us to rejoice in evil, even when it happens to an enemy. "Do not gloat over the day of your brother in the day of his misfortune" (Obad 1:12). That's hard, in fact nearly impossible for me.

Years ago I asked God to discipline a neighbor whose outdoor live band kept me awake with my newborn one night. About two years later, I heard her say she hadn't slept a single night for six months because of her new baby. Needless to say, I reacted like Edom.

We want vengeance (disguised as justice), which God says belongs to him alone. I'm glad I never prayed as Job did, or I would be in undiminished misery. Job asks God to curse him, "If I have rejoiced at the ruin of him who hated me, or exulted when evil overtook him (I have not let my mouth sin by asking for his life with a curse)" (Job 31:29-30). We might rationalize our actions and attitude as a push for fairness. However, the Bible says, "Beloved, never avenge yourselves, but leave it to the wrath of God, for it is written, 'Vengeance is Mine, I will repay, says the Lord'" (Rom 12:19).

My child

When our son rode a bus to a school, a younger boy sat next to him and poked our son in the ribs every day. It would have been easy for my husband to advise him to take vengeance by either punching him or reporting him to the bus driver. Personally, I myself wanted to punch the kid so hard that he would never forget it. But my husband took out the Bible: "If anyone slaps you on the right cheek, turn to him the other also . . . Love your enemies and pray for those who persecute you"(Matt 5:39, 44). My husband advised our son to give a candy bar to the boy each day. We prayed, but I thought my husband was being naive. Within the week, the boy stopped harassing our son. God's ways are not our ways.

My thoughts

It is not always hatred or vengeance that motivates us. Sometimes it is a wish deep in our heart, born out of envy, that someone else would fail. I find this happens not so often for my own advancement, as for my children's. "If he got injured, then my son could play that position." On occasion, I can hide murder under the guise of God's glory. "If that non-Christian team failed in the academic panel, and my son's team did well, it would show how God blesses his people." All of these scenarios according to God are a form of hatred, tantamount to murder.

Or, we may "merely neglect" life, even life in ourselves. How many times have we wished we wouldn't see the next day. We have grown weary of life with all its trials, grieved over a lost loved one so we didn't want to go on, hated our failures that had harmed others, or felt we had become a meaningless annoyance. I have many times. These all stem from lies, accusations, and attacks from Satan. His goal is to wipe out any vestige of God, including people made in his image. He was a murderer from the beginning (John 8:44). To listen to him would make us an accomplice to the devil's wicked designs.

We cannot just passively obey this command by not harming ourselves or others. God condemned Edom for passive apathy. "On the day you stood aloof, on the day strangers carried off his wealth . . . you were like one of them" (Obad 1:11). We are not merely to stay our hand from murder, but we are to "live peaceably with all men," overcoming evil with good (Rom 12:18, 21). We are to conscientiously preserve life. For example, why does God command fences to be built around Israelite house roofs (Deut 22:8)? The protection of life, not just from probable danger, but even from possible danger is expected of us.

The principle became a proverb in our home for our sons. "Yes I know there is a low probability of a bear attacking your tent in the backyard. But there is a possibility. So I am not packing any food. You will have to come back into the house to eat." Possibility trumps even the smallest percentage of probability.

Christ

Neither does just trying to avoid active or passive murder fulfill this commandment. God requires a positive action from me because life is inestimably precious in another way. In addition to creation making man valuable as God's image bearer, a second major act of God gives life value: redemption.

Sometimes I ask my Sunday school students, "How much are you worth?" Answer: "The life of the Son of God." "How much is he worth?" Answer: "An inestimable, infinite amount." "So how much are you worth?" He became a man and sacrificed himself for mankind. How dare we devalue our worth or that of anyone else? How dare we devalue the life of God?

If Jesus died to give us eternal life, and he himself is that life, we should imitate him. We should not only negatively not murder, but we should positively give life. This means giving life physically and spiritually. We are called to protect, preserve and promote life, including the weak, sickly, disabled, unborn, and elderly. We are called to produce children, image bearers. That means babies, but it also means evangelism. Giving the word of life to others, who believe by faith and are born into God's family, is the opposite of killing.

The opposite of murderous hatred is love. The opposite of destroying life is creating life. To actually obey this commandment, I must love and promote life in others. I'm trying to learn to speak highly of others, both to their face and to other people and not just be quiet or scoff in silence. But I fail repeatedly. So, from my son brandishing his pocket knife to my hurtful, vengeful thoughts, our home is a virtual Alcatraz for murderers. Praise God that Jesus opened the jail and gates, as he did for Peter, and set us free. Now I am legally considered not guilty, because he stood in my place condemned. Now there is no condemnation for those who are in Christ Jesus (Rom 8:1). Along with the murderers Moses and David and Paul, I am justified by faith.

Jesus as God's perfect child never murdered, or had any vengeful thought. In fact he prayed for his Father to forgive those who were killing him (Luke 23:34). Out of him flowed the opposite of death. From him sprang all physical and spiritual life. "All things were made through him, and without him was not any thing made that was made. In him was life, and the life was the light of men" (John 1:3-4). Then he gave that life to us and made us springs of life. "But whoever drinks of the water that I will give him will never be thirsty forever. The water that I will give him will become in him a spring of water welling up to eternal life" (John 4:14).

All this comes from Jesus, the one I put to death, the one I murdered. Yet, God has declared me justified. Although I am a criminal, a killer of God's Son and stand condemned, he pronounces me free from guilt. Is it because I never sinned? No. Is it because God is a nice, cuddly grandfather who overlooks my mistakes? No. The Bible says, "The Lord is slow to anger, abounding in love and forgiving sin and rebellion, yet he does not leave the guilty unpunished" (Num 14:18). How could I be pronounced by the judge of the universe as not guilty, even though I am guilty? I killed God's Son. I murdered others by thought, word, and deed.

What has happened? The great exchange. Jesus came into my death row prison cell, let me out, and then was condemned and killed instead of me. Jesus took my guilty sentence and gave me his not-guilty status, his status of righteousness: "Jesus our Lord, who was delivered up for our trespasses and raised for our justification" (Rom 4:24-25). I was let go, a freed citizen of God's kingdom, because "we are justified by his grace as a gift, through the redemption that is in Christ Jesus" (Rom 3:24). I am justified, counted as not guilty, because another took my death sentence, "so that he might be just and the justifier of the one who has faith in Jesus" (Rom 3:26). According to the requirements of God's law (eternal death for sin against an eternal God), I am no longer guilty. In God's court of law, it is just as if I had never sinned. Another one, a second Adam, died for my sins because of his great love for me. When I stand before God's judgment throne, I will be wrapped in the robe of Jesus who will stand with me and declare me not guilty. He died for me. He is my justifier, my perfect savior. He is the Creator and source of all life, the tree of life itself, from whom flow rivers of living water. Because he is my justification, I am included in that everlasting life. Now I can overflow with eternal life and nourish others with that life. "whoever believes in me, as the Scripture has said, 'Out of his heart will flow rivers of living water'" (John 7:38).

Response

How can I be that tributary of life today? Today, if I ignore all the failures, I could see a little trickle of life nourishment being expressed. Well, quite literally I hooked up my car jumper cables to a dead car battery, which then came to life! I prepared meals, fed myself, fed the cat, watered the plants. I read God's word and later providentially was able to cite an application from it for a festering sin in my friend's church. I started to envy my friend who phoned about her recent trip, but God gave me a love for her that rejoiced in her blessing, and I repented. A mailed note arrived from a friend who has lived in the shadow of death for fifteen years. I prayed for her life and her family, and again repented of my ingratitude for life. I prayed with my family for life in other parts of the world where spiritual and physical life is tenuous at best. I bit my tongue several times to keep back remarks that would have hurt, scarred, mocked, or injured. That surprised me how God's power proved so much greater than my incessant sin. Hopefully, I reminded a friend that as a Christian she was more important than the Hollywood stars she met in the photos. The "stars" should have been honored to be in her presence. Not a very spectacular day, was it? It was more like a couple dribbles of living water running down a dirty window pane, than Niagara Falls. Yet God poured his life into me and rejoices in such small reflections of himself in each of us.

7

The Seventh Commandment

Jesus Redeems

You shall not commit adultery. (Exod 20:14)

What is the meaning of adultery?

THIS IS THE ONE commandment that seems so clear, doesn't it? Either you did it or you didn't. Either you are intimate with your spouse exclusively, or you aren't (Deut 22:22). But knowing our perverse hearts and how many ways we could try detours, God defined the boundaries. You marry one wife (or, by implication, one husband) (Matt 19:4–6, 9; 1 Tim 3:2,12; Titus 1:6). You are not intimate with that person before marriage, which would be the sin of fornication (Exod 22:16; Deut 22:23–29, 1 Cor 6:9). "Engaged" does not mean "married," so there are no early privileges to be taken. You are not intimate with anyone else except your spouse (Lev 20:10). You are not intimate with close relatives, people of your own sex, or animals (Lev 18:6–17, 22; 20:13; Rom 1:18–27). You may not divorce or desert that spouse, except for adultery or abandonment (Matt 5:31–32; 1 Cor 7:15). A child of God may not marry an unbeliever, which would be like a living person playing with a dead person (2 Cor 6: 7–18). Simple, straight forward, right?

The circumstances of the situation weren't quite so clear-cut for my girlfriend's suspicious husband. Due to a situation involving military deployment, he and my girlfriend spent their honeymoon at her childhood home. One night, the new husband awoke to hear his bride talking in her sleep to "Ricky," which was not his own name. "Come on in, Ricky. It's okay. Come on. Aren't you the sweetest!" The next morning, he casually asked her, "Who's 'Ricky'?" After thinking awhile, she remembered the family's outdoor pet raccoon. In the night, she used to coax him up the tree into her window in order to play with him. If only all such misunderstandings were so innocent!

The commandment is clear but the sin in us asks: "So, how far can I go without breaking this law? Can I date non-Christians especially to evangelize them, gaze at real or unreal photos, hold hands, kiss, hug, touch, or unclothe?" When was the last time someone in the youth group asked, "How can I be more pure?" Everyone wants to slide to the lowest level with everyone else. The world squeezes us in. The Bible says, "Bad company corrupts good morals" (1 Cor 15:33). That bad company may include movies, music, magazines, phones, or internet images. Culture doesn't help here.

Parents everywhere know the physical dangers abounding in society, and the devastation that breaking this commandment brings. In particular, Christian parents know the results of breaking the seventh law, which are made clear by Scripture. Our honor and wealth go to another (Prov 5:9–11). Our mind and reasoning become debased (Rom 1:28). We should be shunned from Christian fellowship (1 Cor 5:11). We have no inheritance in God's kingdom (1 Cor 6:9–10). God will take vengeance on us for those we hurt (1 Thess 4:2–8). Our soul is destroyed (Prov 6:32–33). Our path leads to death (Prov 2:16–20). We end up in the lake of fire in eternal death (Prov 5:11, Jude 7).

My child

We each know the dire consequences and try to hedge our child's waywardness with rules. In our family, these had to be applied much earlier than we ever foresaw. One day when our son returned from kindergarten, he declared, "I've found the girl I'm going to marry."

"Tell me about her. Has she given her heart to Jesus? Is she a Christian? You know God says you can only marry a Christian."

"I don't know. I'll ask her tomorrow."

Running into my arms after school the next day, he cried, "She is not a Christian!"

"Oh, honey, I am so sorry," and I hugged him tighter as he continued.

"She is Jewish."

"What did you say to her?"

"I told her she was going to hell."

Well, that was the first of many conversations. Surrounding both sons with another layer of wisdom, we taught them they should not even think about courting or dating until they were able to take care of a girl. Can you give her a house, or food, or pay for her medical bills? Then there's no use pursuing her until you can. God has his choice and his time for you.

Actions

We can also hedge our own ways physically. God tells us to make no provision for the flesh and its desires, but rather to put on Christ (Rom 13:14). We can think ahead. When have we failed? When will that situation present itself again? How can we prevent the situation? We can resolve in Christ's power to present our bodies as living sacrifices to him (Rom 12:1–2). Then the God of grace strengthens us to glorify him in all things (Rom 8:28), and we are able to "put to death ... sexual immorality, impurity, passion, evil desire ..." (Col 3:5).

God gives us weapons for fighting this battle. One is the fruit of the Holy Spirit in self-control. Did you know that when you tell your toddler not to touch the vase and then smack his hand when he does, that you have helped keep him from sexual sin (1 Thess 4:3–5)? He has begun to learn to say no to himself and control his body. Suddenly the toddler exhortation, "Keep your hands to yourself," grows in its implications for lifetime purity, both for him and us. In fact, God condemns a couple of older girls in the Bible who don't tell men this simple pre-school rule (Ezek 23:1–21).

What about once we are already in a bad situation? What else can we do? God told us to hide his word in our heart so we might not sin against him (Ps 119:9–11). We can use appropriate memorized verses. I remember my sister finding strength in the verse "If you love me, you will keep my commandments" (John 14:15). We can put on the full armor of God and know how to use it (Eph. 6:10–17). For example, with each son, we acted out some scenarios of a girl flirting with him and then had him act out the biblical response (Prov 2:16).

In the midst of the temptation, we know God has promised an escape (1 Cor 10:13). We can look for it. We can and should flee, even physically like Joseph (Gen 39:7–20, 2 Tim 2:22, 1 Cor 6:18). In fact, God commands us to run away. "Flee from sexual immorality" (1 Cor 6:18). We can run away mentally, too. God and his word are our safe house, our refuge. "For the weapons of our warfare are not of the flesh but have divine power to destroy strongholds. We . . . take every thought captive to obey Christ" (2 Cor 10:4–5). We can have a list of good things to think about (Phil 4:8). This was an escape King David could have used as he looked from his roof.

My actions

I remember once in college when my girlfriend's unsaved father gave me a ride. Suddenly, he pulled off the road and began to proposition me. I froze. I began to pray, and God caused me to begin witnessing to him and brought many verses to mind. The man finally took me safely to my school, and then a couple months later gave his life to Jesus. He didn't need me; he needed Jesus.

Why can't we just do as we please with our bodies? Our bodies do not belong to us, but God owns them. "You are not your own, for you were bought with a price. So glorify God in your body" (1 Cor 6:19–20). He made us, and he bought us. He lives in his children. That means our bodies actually become his temple (1 Cor 6:15–17, 19; 2 Cor 6:16). When we commit adultery, we sin against God, against others, and even against our own body. "Every other sin a person commits is outside the body, but the sexually immoral person sins against his own body" (1 Cor 6:18). God demonstrates his love for us—body and soul—in the resurrection, because God became incarnate in a human body and will resurrect our bodies (Rom 8:23).

God is not interested in how far we can go toward looking like the world, but how far we can go in looking like Jesus. That is one reason why he warns us in this area of purity to not even look like we are doing evil. "Abstain from every form [appearance] of evil" (Eph 5:3; 1 Thess 5:22). That is why pastors and professors have windows in their office doors, why our neighbor stays with her sister when an overseas male boards at her home, why I don't go into a home with a meal while the wife is gone. Avoid any *appearance* of evil, God says.

At one point, we had to warn our son that although others (even Christians) found it pragmatic to share apartment expenses among mixed sexes, he could not. It is better to spend more money than to have mud slung on the name of Christ. Not even a *hint* of sexual impropriety, the Bible warns. It is said that Billy Graham long ago determined to never ride in a car with any woman except his wife. Why? For the love of Christ, and for the sake of his glory.

One time I confided in my godly girlfriend on the phone that a pastor whom I had dated when we were unmarried classmates was coming to visit. She advised me to meet him in a public place, but he was already on his way. So she told me to keep her on the phone and leave the phone nearby where she would pray and be an unseen presence. She taught me to guard my ways and to think creatively about hedges. God promised that there are always means of escape from temptations.

Thoughts

This commandment forbidding adultery pertains to our physical life, but also to our thought life. Jesus said, "You have heard that it was said, 'You shall not commit adultery,' but I say to you that everyone who looks at a woman with lustful intent has already committed adultery with her in his heart" (Matt 5:27–28). Adultery begins with lust. Lust begins with wanting more, not being content with what God has apportioned to us. Lust begins in the heart, seeps into the mind, and culminates in action. Each step is part of the whole of adultery, both root and branch.

Thought temptations come in many forms. Satan knows that a Christian's testimony and work can be publicly destroyed by this sin. That is why he most frequently attacks church leaders at this point. One of my classmates found this particularly challenging as a missionary, sitting by a fire pit across from several topless native women. Also, the late president of my seminary, a godly former pastor, once testified in chapel. When an attractive young woman came to his office for guidance, he welcomed her. But, he confessed, he had so enjoyed her company that he prolonged the number of counseling appointments necessary to deal with her problem. He warned the young men to guard their hearts and minds in Christ Jesus (Phil 4:7).

My thoughts

Most of these physical and mental temptations mainly affect men. But what about women? No one ever told me that just imagining being kissed by a boy was wrong (Ezek 23:14–16). My own teenage beaus were usually stars from TV shows. I didn't really know if they were married in real life, nor did I care. I didn't know if they drank, smoked, went to church, or lived immorally. I only knew the TV image that I embraced in my own imaginary world.

Such relationships circumvent apparent sin and avoid rejection. The pretend boyfriend can be a hero, a gentleman, a gallant protector or whatever else I want my robot to be. But that is exactly what he becomes. The person is dehumanized, detached from reality. He never sins, and I live in a paradise of my own making. In this way, I abuse him as a person, ignore his marriage vows, and reject God's separate plans for his life and mine. It is perhaps a form of female pornography where, instead of lusting after body parts, we lust after the relationship. We seek to live vicariously through the heroine as she faints into her boyfriend's strong, caring arms. Eugene O'Neill once said "Obsessed by a fairy tale, we spend our lives searching for a magic door and a lost kingdom of peace."[1] We have exchanged the Creator for the creation (Rom 1:25).

How do we stop thoughts? Martin Luther once said of temptation that you can't stop the birds from flying over your head. But you can stop them from making a nest in your hair. We can't stop lustful thoughts from presenting themselves to us, but we can stop them from taking root. Sermons often point out that David did not just grab Bathsheba. He contemplated her from his roof. Instead of taking his gaze away and filling his mind and sight with other ideas, he lingered. The temptation took root.

My child

I wanted to keep my own sons pure. Although I grew up with only one sister, I had read about men 's temptations. Whenever a magazine came to the home with some sultry cover, it immediately got put in the trash. We had set up a list of rules, with suggestions from the boys when they were young, as to how to judge if something were God honoring. These were applied especially to TV, movies, books, and games. That list had filtered out much of the world's filth. But one day I found my pre-teen son lingering

---

1. O'Neill, http://www.brainyquote.com/citation/quotes/quotes/e/eugeneone163822.html?ct=Eugene+O%27Neill.

over the lingerie section in the Sears catalog. If a squirrel had flown through the window, tied on an apron, and begun washing my dishes, I wouldn't have been more surprised. Where did that come from? I was horrified. I thought I had been so careful. Can such vileness actually exist in my innocent child? Not in my child! But again I had not taken into account the fallenness of the heart, which paraded itself without any outside provocation. All the rules and fences in the world are useless when the heart is twisted.

Attitude

Our heart constantly creates idols. The idol might be a person or it might be a feeling of security, worth, or love. If men admire us, seek us out, compliment us, we feel loved. Somehow we think God's love is not enough. So we want men to want us. We have equated desire with love. We have turned love into a mere feeling, rather than a daily commitment, a covenant of sacrificial devotion. Such shallow shadows of God, who is love himself! We reject the one who gave his life for us, in favor of a passing platitude from someone that makes us feel better. "He who did not spare his own Son but gave him up for us all, how will he not also with him graciously give us all things (Rom 8:32)?

My attitude

I didn't believe God would give me a husband. I had thirteen roommates get married while I was living with them. Ask me how to arrange a wedding, any wedding. I've seen them all from outdoor, flowered fields to cavernous cathedrals, from glued-on sequins to Boston boutiques (where they produce a copy of their designer original for your gratis doll). If you go to seminary where there are only seventeen girls, out of several hundred men, and you still don't get married, you tend to lose hope. I did not trust God to love me with his best, with himself. I was his tearful, petulant bride.

The Seventh Commandment

I was born with a heart murmur. We all were. Not the physical kind, but the spiritual kind like the Israelites in the wilderness. I murmur, mumble, grumble, and complain against my Lord. I am not content with what God gave me in himself. How can I be so unfaithful, so unbelieving, actually thinking that a job, a child, a husband, a pet, a movie, a book, a trip, or an award might fill what is lacking in my estranged relationship with God? I throw my love favors, like Mardi Gras necklaces, on all kinds of idols. It is my own sin that has distanced me from the cup of his fulfilling marriage covenant love. What can be done? To grow out of love with the world, I must grow deeper in love with God.

Little do we believe that God alone is our true sweetheart. Yet, God marries us when he comes into our heart. He already became engaged to us, expressing his intent toward us in eternity past, by writing our names in his book of life (Ps 139:16; Jer 31:3). We belong to him. His covenant vow is "I will be your God and you will be my people." This is so deep that he created us man and woman and gave us marriage so we might begin to understand the mystery of our union with him (Eph. 5:32). Just as a man and woman become one in marriage, so in a similar way we become united to God (1 Cor 6:15–17). Earthly marriage and heavenly union are so connected in parallelism that covenant breaking is forbidden. Human marriage vows copy God's marriage vows to us. God will never leave us or forsake us, so we must never leave nor forsake our spouse—physically, emotionally, socially, or spiritually. Unfaithfulness to our husband is adultery. Unfaithfulness to God is seen by him as adultery (Jer 3:6–9). We break our human union on pain of death (Lev 20:10). We break our relationship with God on pain of eternal death. We have betrayed our heavenly maker, our husband, by deserting him for the shiny baubles of this world. God equates this with adultery (Jer 3; Ezek 16).

Christ

The remedy must be radical, for the rebellion is radical. Our hearts are intertwined with knots of sin. "But each person is tempted when he is lured and enticed by his own desire. Then desire when it has conceived gives birth to sin, and sin when it is fully grown brings forth death" (Jas 1:13–15). Then these lusts war against our soul (1 Pet 2:11). God calls them idols. "Put to death ... sexual immorality, impurity, passion, evil desire, and covetousness, which is idolatry" (Col 3:5). I need my heart changed by the only one who is able; the only one who not only knows how to love perfectly, but is love itself.

Christ came as the perfect lover. He always remained in covenant with his Father, fulfilling even the pact of death agreed upon in eternity past (John 17:4; Gal 4:4). His love never wandered, never weakened, never wished for someone or something else. His willing love, as in 1 Cor 13, was not self-seeking but always rejoiced in the truth. He never proved unfaithful to God (John 4:34; 5:30). "I always do the things that are pleasing to him" (John 8:29). "I seek not my own will but the will of him who sent me" (John 5:30). "I glorified you on earth, having accomplished the work that you gave me to do" (John 17:4).

He also perfectly loved me, his chosen bride, with that covenant love. When he could have said to me, "She is not mine, not my grown up child bride in any way, shape, or form," he did not abandon me. When he could have sent me away with a letter of divorce and a scarlet "A" branded on my forehead, he was both able and willing to save me. He laid down his own life and bought me with his own blood. We can see his love through Hosea. "Go take to yourself a wife of whoredom . . . for the land commits great whoredom by forsaking the Lord" (Hos 1:2). God directs the prophet that when he finds his wife in the arms of another man to buy her back. Hosea is instructed to pursue, plead with, allure, speak tenderly to, forgive, and show mercy to his wayward wife. Here is true love. Here is our God. Yes, he bought me, redeemed me, paid the bride price for me—a prostitute to the world. How much did you and I cost? All of the blood, poured out on the altar by Christ the groom: "Who gave himself for us to redeem us from all lawlessness and to purify for himself a people for his own possession . . ." (Titus 2:14), "knowing that you were ransomed . . . not with perishable things such as silver or gold, but with the precious blood of Christ" (1 Pet 1:19).

God bought us. He redeemed us from the world to which we had given ourselves. No amount of money could pay for my bottomless debt in hell. Not even giving my own blood, either by death or by living in slavery through my work, self-flagellation, or mourning could ransom me. But Christ did it. He paid it all in full. ". . . the account is settled; the handwriting is nailed to the cross; the receipt is given, and we are debtors to God's justice no longer."[2] Jesus Christ is our redemption, our payment for the just amount of suffering we owed: ". . . the man Christ Jesus, who gave himself as a ransom for all" (I Tim 2:5–6). Our bridegroom Jesus has bought us with the price of his own life. Now we walk down the aisle toward him, not in filthy rags, but like Joshua the priest, in a gown of snow-white glory made by Christ himself. "Having cleansed her by the washing of water with the word, so that he might present the church [us] to himself in splendor, without spot or wrinkle or any such thing, that she might be holy and without blemish" (Eph 5:26–27).

Christ is interceding for us and his desire is for us to be holy (1 Thess 4:1–7; Heb 4:14–16). By the power of the Holy Spirit at work in us, that resurrection power of Christ, we can stop behaving like a devil, toss off darkness and kill sin (Rom 13:12–14; Col 3:5). We can start behaving like Christ himself (2 Cor 5:17; Eph 4:22; Phil 3:16). In that way we are loving our beloved, our Lord (John 14:15).

Response

So what do I do when Mr. Darcy presents himself literally or figuratively? Pray for God to create in you a clean heart before you get tempted. Pray in the midst of temptation. Pray for a clean heart when you have sinned. Repent and be forgiven (Ps 51; Matt 5:29–30). Pray to be made new, and for the power and guilt of sin

---

2. Spurgeon, *Morning and Evening*, 68.

to be removed by Christ (1 Cor 6:9–11). Pray this both for you and for your child.

How do we find scarecrows to shoo away these birds? The means of grace mentioned above provide help. In addition, we can set our face like flint to obey God. Job made a covenant with his eyes not to look lustfully at a woman (Job 31:1). Following his example, we taped a sign over our TV for several years, "I will walk with integrity of heart within my house; I will not set before my eyes anything that is worthless" (Ps 101:3). Adulterous lust usually enters our lives through the eyes.

One of our teen relatives closed the door to mental onslaughts when he went with a sports team to compete in another state. The coach told the boys to walk to the end of town to see the fireworks that night. On the way, they passed a strip bar where the team wanted to go in. Our relative had a Christian friend on the team with whom he had memorized Bible verses as a kid. That friend urged, "Let's go in with them. Then they will see that we are regular guys, and they will be more apt to listen to our testimony." Our relative refused, stating he wanted to stay pure, and then went on to the fireworks alone. That night in the hotel, with lights out, the other boys, convicted of their guilt, started asking him what it meant to be pure and who is God and how do you please him. So God blessed his resolve to keep his mind pure.

So today when I want to revisit the strong face of a hero from last night's movie, I can think instead about how Jesus is that hero and more for me. When I see an internet photo of my perpetually eighteen-year-old friend who is a mother of two grown children and compare that with the two pounds my matronly frame gained overnight, I will determine not to despair. For I am loved with an everlasting love. When I see a provocative photo in a magazine, I can pray for the salvation of that person. I can meditate while cooking on how the beauty outside my window shows the lavish love of my beloved for me. "Hear, O daughter, and consider . . . the king will desire your beauty. Since he is your lord, bow to him" (Ps 45:10–11). I can bask in the love of my heavenly maker, redeemer, and husband.

8

The Eighth Commandment

Jesus Adopts

> You shall not steal. (Exod 20:15)

REMEMBER THE CHURCH YOUTH joke? "What was the first game in the Bible? Baseball—because it starts 'in the big inning.' How was the game played? Eve stole first. Adam stole second. Abraham sacrificed. And the prodigal son came home."

It's funny, but it's true. Yes, Eve stole first. God planted his own trees in the Garden of Eden, told Adam and Eve to take care of them, and that they could eat from any of the trees they wanted, except this one tree—the tree of the knowledge of good and evil. That was God's tree like all the others. But this one was his alone. Eve believed the serpent's lie, disobeyed God, and stole the fruit. To make matters worse, she gave some of the stolen goods to her husband as well. Ever since then, all their children have had the hearts of thieves. Unfortunately that included my children.

My child

When one son was still small enough to ride in a grocery cart, I caught him eating grapes from the bin. "Did you pay for those? No? I didn't pay for them either. They belong to the storekeeper. We have taken something that belonged to him. Now we need to pay him." We found the manager. My son confessed to him what he had done while I pulled out my wallet. Years later my other son, as a teen, confessed to having taken a candy bar from the local pharmacy when very little. The guilt carried all those years was expunged in a similar way.

What does it mean to steal?

Stealing tends to fall into two categories, namely what is seen and what is unseen. Property is seen. This is someone's house, purse, money, car, land, clothing, pet, or husband. We learn quite young that we cannot carry off another child's ball without consequences. When King Ahab wanted Naboth's vineyard, his wife stole it through murder and collusion. God declared that she and her husband would die, dogs would have their blood, and none of their sons would survive. God has prescribed legal consequences for thievery, which range from capital punishment for kidnapping to equal repayment (Exod 21:16; 22:1–4, 7; Deut 24:7). Joseph, Moses, Naaman's servant girl, Daniel, Shadrach, Meshach, Abednego, and Esther were all stolen from their families.

    Stealing can happen in an unfair exchange of goods. There's the old joke about the store owner who tells the employee, "Take that shirt and mark it up $10 and down $2." Both the buyer and the seller can be guilty, though. For the cover of *Saturday Evening Post*, Leslie Thrasher depicted a seller weighing a chicken on a scale, with his finger secretly pushing down on the scale pan. Unknown to him, the little old lady who was buying the chicken had her finger under the scale pan pushing up. Each person attempted to swindle the other person. God forbids such exchanges in Deut 25:13–16.

Stealing can happen passively as when the owner of a cow allows it to "escape" into the neighbor's corn field. God designates a punishment for such neglect, whether purposely perpetrated or not (Exod 22:5). We might apply this to suburbia when a cat is allowed to prowl under a neighbor's bird feeder or when dogs relieve themselves on other people's property. The Bible also warns against passivity when we find a lost animal (Exod 22:5; 23:4; Deut 22:1–3). Do we try to care for an animal until an owner can be reached or put up signs in the neighborhood indicating that we found this pet? Other things wander away, like coats, hairclips, or keys. Do we care for other people's missing property until they find it? Do we try to notify them?

My child

School had been over for a month, so the boys had settled into a relaxed summer routine. I could finally clear out papers from last year and assess which supplies needed to be replaced. When I opened a bag by my son's desk, I suddenly saw a collection of pink, white, and brown erasers. Knowing that we had never bought these, I asked him where they came from. Well, it started out with someone telling him he could take an eraser from the lost and found box, since no one had claimed it. Then he took others, sometimes ones he found in the box, sometimes ones left on a desk. Didn't he know that was stealing? No, he thought that the principle was "finders keepers, losers weepers." The Bible says sin is sin even if we are unaware of it (Lev 5:17). We prayed and discussed God's laws. So new erasers were bought with chore money and given with an apology the next fall along with returning all the stolen property. This couldn't have been my child, could it? God, did he have to sin in front of you and all his friends like this?

My actions

My mother fondly remembers a similar scenario from my own childhood. I was playing about a half block up the street from our house with my friend Judy. As she started to walk home with me, she suggested I take a couple flowers home from her yard. As we passed the next house, she remarked that her neighbor sometimes gave them flowers. Why not add a couple more to my handful? She wouldn't mind. We seemed to know most of the neighbors between her house and mine and were convinced of their generosity. By the time I came home, I had a huge bouquet of daffodils, tulips, and hyacinths. I thought my mother would be so very pleased with my surprise gift for her. Instead, she opened the door stunned, asking where I had gotten the blooms. When I told her, she promptly took me by the hand and reversed my route, stopping at each pilfered property to allow me to apologize. I, like my sons, had been a thief.

On the fringe of outright stealing is borrowing without intent to return, or without concern for the other person's use of his own property. A woman in our neighborhood once spotted an unusual book of essays on our bookshelf and asked if she could borrow it to read. After a month, a year, two years, the book had not been returned. I had not been able to find a replacement copy anywhere. Finally, after three years, the lady walked in, casually commenting that she had found this book that she had borrowed "a couple of months ago." We were deprived of consulting that book for three years, nor could we lend it or share it with anyone else. God has consequences for irresponsible borrowers (Ps 37:21).

Money

Money and property can be taken not only from individuals but also from groups of individuals. Taxes take away money earned by people. Sometimes these taxes are collected for everyone's use, such as paying snow plows to clear streets. Sometimes taxes are amassed by individuals. Imelda Marcos, wife of the Filipino president, had no shoes as a child, so she collected hundreds as an adult. Mrs. Marcos used the money from her impoverished citizens for her shoes, money that was supposed to be spent for protecting the lives of her people. We call this a misappropriation of funds. God does not condemn her wealth, but the manner in which she attained it and how she used it. Justice does not mean that everyone gets the same amount of money, as can be seen in God's instruction that the first born is to get a double inheritance (Deut 21:17). But it does mean that property owned should not be unfairly removed. The point of this commandment is not just desiring something that is not ours, but unrighteously taking it.

Most of us never bear the responsibility, or temptation, of handling the money of others. However, money due to others may stick to our palms. Do we want to return money to a store when we are undercharged? Do we give the authorities the taxes or building-permit monies required? Once when my husband was buying a car privately, the seller suggested that a lower amount of sale be registered, so the tax would be lower. My husband explained that as a Christian, he could not do that. What about employing babysitters and handymen? Do we pay workmen on time rather than squeezing out a couple more dollars of interest for ourselves from the bank? Have we acquired money at the expense of other people who were harmed?

For example, in Nehemiah's day, men lent their money at such high rates of interest that the people were impoverished by the usury (Neh 5:1-13). Did we receive something that we should not have been given or that really belonged to others? Did we take some money donated to a specific project and use it differently to pay for other things besides that project? So, for example, when the youth group has a car wash to raise money for missions and there is money left over, does the extra money go into a missions fund for next year, or is it used in some other way than intended by the donor?

Next to sexual sin, stealing is the most common form of satanic attack on Christian leaders. Once a leader fails in this area, he rarely regains any influence for the gospel. Achan stole silver, gold, and a beautiful cloak from Jericho. Rachel robbed her father of his household idols. David stole a piece of Saul's robe, then later regretted it and returned it. Judas took money from the disciples' common purse. Ananias and Sapphira pocketed proceeds from a sale that they had dedicated to the Lord. God says, "Do not be deceived: neither the sexually immoral . . . nor thieves . . . nor swindlers will inherit the kingdom of God" (1 Cor 6:10).

We can also steal money from God. He owns all the property and money in the world. But he has gifted some of that to people for a while. We are stewards who on judgment day must give a report about how we invested his resources (Matt 25:15–28). Although everything is his, just like in the Garden of Eden, He specifically claims one part as his very own. He calls that part the "tithe." One tenth of all we receive has his name on it. To use it for ourselves, "borrow" it, or otherwise allocate it is stealing. "Will man rob God? Yet you are robbing me. But you say, 'How have we robbed You?' In your tithes and contributions. You are cursed with a curse, for you are robbing me" (Mal 3:8–9). On the other hand, if we do give him his tithe, he promises us a blessing (Mal 3:10).

Attitude of greed

Greed starts with the first toddler's cry of "Mine!" as a toy is pulled from another child. We have all done this. Unfortunately, this scenario etched itself forever onto a family Christmas movie when one son received a fire engine that the other wanted. Earlier I remember being pregnant and glaring at my husband when he started to take the last helping of food, thinking: "That was for my baby. Don't you dare touch it." But God corrects our sinful view, "Lay up for yourself treasures in heaven, where neither moth nor rust destroys and where thieves do not break in and steal" (Matt 6:20).

As with my son's eraser collection, rationalization of sin often sets in for all of us. We might consider that taking money from a parent isn't really stealing since it is all in the family. God disagrees (Prov 28:24). Or we might reason: "If my roommate were here, she would definitely let me use this; after all, she let me use it in the past." "I really do deserve this, and people would give it to me if only they knew me and how much I need it." We have this propensity for greed, ownership, self-indulgence, and control. As we grow, the form may change into subtler varieties, but it is still the same sin. We set aside treasures on earth that disintegrate along with our heart (Matt 6:19–21). In truth, we own nothing, but are only stewards at this moment of history. As Elisabeth Elliot observes, "What God gives us is not necessarily 'ours' but only ours to offer back to him, ours to relinquish, ours to lose, ours to let go of, if we want to be our true selves."[1]

My attitude of greed

As I drove past that lovely free chair at the curb, I was tempted. "Mine is old," I thought. "What if we have more guests than chairs someday? That one is so much prettier than mine. Maybe my son could use it."

Owning more things may make us feel secure, but that is unbelief. We have stopped believing that God will provide for all our needs according to his riches in Christ Jesus (Phil 4:19). Like Eve, we sinfully reject God's promise to not keep anything from us that is good. "He who did not spare his own Son but gave him up for us all, how will he not also with him graciously give us all things?" (Rom 8:32; see Ps 84:11). Do we really trust God? Do we in fact think that the one who made us doesn't know what we need? "But if God so clothes the grass of the field, which today is alive and tomorrow is thrown into the oven, will he not much more clothe you, O you of little faith? . . . Your heavenly Father knows that you need them all. But seek first the kingdom of God and his righteousness, and all these things will be added to you" (Matt 6:30, 33). If we really believed him, then stealing would lose its attraction. By faith, we trust in who God is—all powerful, sovereign, and love itself. God's very name is Shaddai ("all powerful").

---

1. Elliot, *Passion and Purity*, https://www.goodreads.com/quotes/search?utf8=%E2%9C%93&q=ours+to+offer+back+to+him&commit=Search

Have you heard the joke about the exceedingly rich man who got to the pearly gates? He asked if he could bring something with him. The doorkeeper told him this was not the usual practice but he would give him permission to bring up one suitcase of whatever he wanted. The wealthy man returned home, inventoried his belongings and decided to fill the suitcase with gold bars. Back at the gate, the curious doorkeeper asked him what he brought. Proudly the man opened his suitcase. The doorkeeper exclaimed, "Why did you bring street paving stones?"

The man in the joke forgot that true treasure does not consist in things, but in unseen valuables like life itself. These unseen things can be stolen also: reputation, opportunity, ideas, time, strength, friendship, peace, love, gratitude, and honor. Clearly, more can be stolen than just money or property. We mentioned in the last chapter the possibility of stealing someone's affection or a spouse. Some, like Jeremiah who was warned not to prophesy, had their jobs stolen (Jer 11:21). Amnon stole the purity of his half-sister. Absalom stole the hearts of the people away from his father. Sanballat and Tobiah stole peaceful security from the Jewish workers. Jacob wanted Esau's blessing and stole it through deception.

Time

More commonly, daily robberies are committed against time. Did you ever chat with someone so long that their family was neglected?

My words

Recently, I conversed with a student in the summer for a long time. Finally she told me that she had to take an online test within the hour. I was so ashamed. I had stolen her study time and maybe her grade.

Work, which encompasses time and life energy, can be stolen by both employers and employees. To withhold fair payment for services or not to pay someone on time is forbidden by God (Lev

19:13; Deut 24:14; 1 Cor 9:9; 1 Tim 5:18). Did you ever "forget" to tip your waiter, your employee?

But employees can also steal time and life from their boss. They are commanded to do their work as to the Lord God himself, not withholding strength or concentration (Eph 6:5–8; Col 3:23). This includes the unique talents and abilities he invested in us. How many times did I know that God gave me a gift that was needed, but I didn't volunteer? Sometimes I excused myself by a mixed motivation of assumed humility or by an unwillingness to add to my busyness. In any case, I was not willing to sacrifice my life or be stressed for the sake of God's kingdom. Sometimes I also allowed my children the same poor escape.

Honor

We can demean people's lives both by what we do and what we say, and by what we don't do and don't say, and thereby steal the happy quality of their life. For example, if someone has falsely accused a school bus driver of abusive language, and I passively say nothing, then the happy disposition of his life in that job may be changed. If a church widow sacrificially decorated tables for a homeless meal, and I speak no word of gratitude, then the encouragement needed for her gifts to blossom may be missing, and as a result her growth is stunted. God's command encompasses stealing that diminishes, in any way, what belongs to another, including sustenance of life.

My child

Because I had to do research and writing for my degree, I always had to carefully study copyright laws and plagiarism regulations. Imagine my shock when I read an interview our son gave, supporting the free replication of artists' music! The idea could have been applied to all art whether it was music, acting, painting, dance moves, writing, dress or architectural design. Where is the honor or recompense for the originator? People we know in the sciences have had projects, grants, discoveries, inventions, and proposals stolen from them, including the monies, job positions, promotions, honor, and family sustenance that would have resulted from them. When my father invented a new machine, the company he worked for claimed the honor, extra revenue, and publicity as their own. Legally, they had a clause that permitted this, but legality and rightness are not always the same. Those who consent to such robbery, even if they don't do it themselves, are also condemned in Scripture (Ps 50:18). God warns us that we can gain the whole world but lose our soul (Mark 8:36).

My attitude

My husband and I were both advertised in the same brochure as speakers. The insert listed my husband's degrees, schools, publications, accomplishments, etc. A bottom line was added, "His wife is also noteworthy." I felt shamed and dishonored. Did I spend eleven years on a PhD, three years writing a book, and months preparing for this lecture for nothing? I didn't want money, but I did want some recognition. I didn't even think about how glad I was that they honored my husband. My pride was justly wounded. I wanted the momentary applause of this world, rather than being happy for the privilege of honoring God in this task.

The greatest theft, the grand heist, is to steal God's glory. Nebuchadnezzar took the glory for building the kingdom of Babylon. God struck him to the ground so that he ate grass like an animal. Herod took to himself the praise reserved for God alone and was immediately struck with worms and died.

When I have received a compliment and not returned it to God, I have stolen from his glory. When he teaches me from his word and through his messengers, and I don't thank him, I have stolen from his due glory. Whenever I see an orange splashed sky and don't praise him for creating it, I have passively stolen praise from him. Whenever my life has not reflected his image, I have lessened his glory. God should be praised with all glory going to him for all things at all times. If a human artist receives honor for his creation, what about the Creator of all things, the artist, originator, and source of all life and ideas?

I once read that Billy Graham received a presidential award and immediately responded, "Another trophy for God." Why would he say that?—"in order that in everything God may be glorified through Jesus Christ" (1 Pet 4:11). After reading that, we encouraged our sons to have a special shelf where they would set their awards as gifts at God's feet. In so doing they could think about offering their lives as the most essential gift.

Christ

In a far greater way, this is what God's Son, Jesus Christ, did. "I have glorified You on earth" (John 17:4). God the Father could look at his Son and say, "Although all others steal my glory, my Son never did that, not my child. He always blesses and sanctifies me. And not only does he honor me uniquely, but he brings the whole universe with him to my throne." "In the promise of new creation, based on Christ's work, we have hope for full restoration of the universe from the damage of all sin. In the suffering of Christ on the cross we have full payment for the punishment of sin as well as vindication of the honor of God."[2] Christ wraps us in a redemptive hug and proudly sets us as rescued treasures before his Father's throne, as part of glorifying God.

Isn't this a marvel! Not only have we been saved from eternal hell fire, but also we are given life, eternal life. God had every right to just make us slaves according to the law, considering we had a debt we could never pay. Yet we are not called slaves, but rather sons. "For you did not receive the spirit of slavery to fall back into fear, but you have received the Spirit of adoption as sons, by whom we cry 'Abba! Father!'" (Rom 8:15). Spurgeon said: "Consider who we were, and what we feel ourselves to be even now when corruption is powerful in us, and you will wonder at our adoption."[3]

---

2. Poythress, *Shadow of Christ*, 128.
3. Spurgeon, *Morning and Evening*, 88.

My Child, His Child

Even though we were condemned by breaking the law, by stealing God's glory, God has redeemed us through his Son. Now we receive the adoption of true sons (Gal 4:4–5). Why would he do this? Because God has set his love on us through his Son. "He predestined us for adoption through Jesus Christ, according to the purpose of his will, to the praise of his glorious grace, with which he has blessed us in the Beloved" (Eph 1:5–6). He has adopted us as his children. Where previously God looked at us declaring, "Not my child, not my people," he now proclaims, "My child, you are mine forever and underneath you are my everlasting arms" (Deut 33:27; Jer 31:3; Hos 1:10). This is his promise: "For as many as did receive him, who believed in his name, he gave the right to become children of God" (John 1:12). If we believe, we are his.

We are not just spared condemnation, nor merely allowed to survive, eking out a meager existence, like reprieved criminals. But we are crowned as children of the king, sharing bread like Mephibosheth at the king's table with his Son. We have been made part of his intimate family through adoption, feasting on his delicacies, showered with his riches. "In him we have obtained an inheritance, having been predestined according to the purpose of him who works all things according to the counsel of his will, so that we who were the first to hope in Christ might be to the praise of his glory" (Eph 1:11–12).

Jesus brings all that he owns, including us, to the Father. "I [Jesus] will tell of your name to my brothers; in the midst of the congregation I will sing your praise . . . Behold, I and the children God has given me" (Heb 1:12,13). God receives us as adopted sons, brothers of his Son. Then Jesus shares all his inheritance as the Son, with us, his brothers. "The Spirit himself bears witness with our spirit that we are children of God, and if children, then heirs—heirs of God and fellow heirs with Christ" (Rom 8:16–17). All that Jesus owns both by original creative right and by redemptive work, he freely gives.

Christ's very own inheritance has been shared with us as adopted sons. We are made co-heirs with him, sons of his heavenly Father (Rom 8:16). It seems absurd in this light that we should ever desire anything or steal anything. "Already you have all you want! Already you have become rich! Without us you have become kings!" (1 Cor 4:8). To Christ belong life, forgiveness, truth, power, peace, the everlasting kingdom. Yet he hands all of this to us. We who stole miserly bits from him, he has welcomed into his home and given everything. Spurgeon adds, "The golden streets of paradise, the pearly gates, the river of life, the transcendent bliss, and the unutterable glory, are, by our blessed Lord, made over to us for our everlasting possession."[4] All that he has he shares with his people: an inheritance imperishable, undefiled, and unfading, kept in heaven for us (1 Pet 1:4).

And the most precious crown jewel of our inheritance as adopted children is God. He has given us himself. "And I will have mercy on No Mercy, and I will say to Not My People, 'You are my people': and he shall say, 'You are my God'" (Hos 2:23). No greater gift could ever be given. No greater honor could he bestow than allowing us to call him "Father." This is the heart of his covenant of love: "I will be your God and you will be my people"; the intensified, intimate, eternal, unwavering promise of himself. He gives us everything that he is—wisdom, power, refuge, savior, counselor, defender, provider, teacher, lover, rescuer, justifier, advocate, healer, leader, Father, Lord. How great the Father's love for us that we should be called the children of God (1 John 3:1)! Being adopted as Christ's brothers, we are now raised up with him and seated with Christ in the heavenly places so that our children and future generations might see the immeasurable riches of his grace in kindness toward us in Christ Jesus (Eph 2:6–7).

Response

We see the church caring for one another in Acts 4:32–37, where "there was not a needy person among them," and where a collection was taken during a famine for "brothers living in Judea" (Acts 11:27–30). Besides neighbors and saints, God instructs us to

---

4. Spurgeon, *Morning and Evening*, 270.

provide for our families (2 Thess 3:10; 1 Tim 5:4,8) and even for ourselves (2 Thess 3:10). All our visible possessions are, after all, just transient things. Like God, we are to set our minds on what is unshakeable. "Temporal things must be treated as temporal things—received, given thanks for, offered back, but enjoyed. They must not be treated like eternal things."[5]

As in Acts, it is not just a matter of not stealing, but of positively doing good. "Let the thief no longer steal, but rather let him labor, doing honest work with his own hands, so that he may have something to share with anyone in need" (Eph 4:28). Jesus told his followers to lend when asked (Matt 5:42), and to care for neighbors (Luke 10:25–37; Rom 13:9–10).

Restitution is part of repentance for this sin. That is what is right. The item must be replaced and the thief must be punished—not merely by replacing what he took. "This punishment for theft reflects on a human level the nature of our obligations to God for our sin. Payment for sin must include both restoration and punishment . . ."[6] Not everything can be equally restored, nor should be. Sometimes five times as much is required in repayment by God; and if repayment cannot be made, the offender might become a slave (Exod 22:1, 4, 5, 7, 10–12; Lev 5:14–16; Num 5:5–8; Prov 6:30–31; Ezek 22:2–3). We need to consider what is a just restitution for our children and ourselves to return in different situations.

The principle behind this eighth commandment is to reflect God's glory and his person. He is gracious, giving everything to those who can return nothing. C. H. Spurgeon noted, "Far superior to the jealousy, selfishness, and greed, which admit of no participation of their advantages, Christ deems his happiness completed by his people sharing it."[7] God gives, so we give. We are to imitate him. That is why he instructed Israelites to cancel debts, return property, welcome gleaners, and care for the poor and orphaned and widows.

How do we fulfill this commandment? We can repent, stop stealing both the seen and the unseen things from people, and

5. Elliot, *Taking Flight*, 93.
6. Poythress, *Shadow of Christ*, 128.
7. Spurgeon, *Morning and Evening*, 270.

give praise where praise is due, whether that be to our child or an employee or a stranger. I have failed in this daily and maybe you have, too. We can work hard with what God has given us in talents and resources. We can do what we are able to do on our own so as not to steal from others, not to exploit others. We can receive God's gifts with thankfulness and multiply them in service for his glory. Our lives can contribute to others, but more importantly, our lives can be sanctified by the Holy Spirit so as to reflect God's glory. The riches of salvation that we bear in bodies of clay can overflow to bless others and give them a taste of eternal life. This includes giving the gospel of life. Did we steal from someone today by not giving them the gospel of life?

This eighth commandment leaves me weak. How can we as his adopted children glorify God in everything at all times and not diminish or steal that glory from him? Yet this is the very thing God has called us to do and enabled us to do by making us his adopted children. When we fail, we can pray God gives us grace to repent and walk on by faith. God promises in Scripture to expunge our guilt, throwing all our sins into the depths of the sea (Mic 7:19). Looking each child in the eye, he loves us perfectly. In perfect love, he promises us that nothing will ever separate us from him (Rom 8: 37-39). When my child fails, I know I must forgive him, show him undeserved mercy, and point him toward the one who made him and adopted him. Why? Because he by grace adopted me as his child, through his Son. We desire to return to our Father all that belongs to him, including his glory and ourselves and our children. May God fulfill his word to us and our families in Hos 1:10, "And in the place where it was said to them, 'You are not my people,' it shall be said to them, 'Children of the living God.'"

9

The Ninth Commandment

Jesus's Righteousness

> You shall not bear false witness against your neighbor.
> (Exod 20:16)

WHILE LOOKING OUT THE window at the birds and squirrels on the ground, pecking up seeds thrown from the bird feeder by a picky blue jay, I noticed something. The birds on guard duty in the nearby tree could sing out a song to warn everyone. But the squirrel only had his fluffy tail to use as a signal banner. Why could birds sing, but not squirrels? What would a squirrel song sound like? Why can people sing and wave their hands and talk and publish warning signs? Why do we even have mouths? Science fiction movies conceive of creatures sporting various anatomical options, like eyes on the forehead. Why do we even need mouths at all? We could just get food through a type of skin osmosis or communicate solely through our hands, couldn't we? But God made our mouths, as he reminded Moses, and made us able to talk (Exod 4:11). That's dangerous. To deny our Creator as Lord or to say that our mouth belongs to us, is to ask for a curse (Ps 12:3–4).

He chose to give us a mouth for a purpose. It serves the double duty of taking in food and giving out speech. He allows us to imitate him in his ability to communicate. In Eph 4:15, he tells us to speak the truth in love and so "grow up in every way into him who is the head, into Christ." Our talking can serve such mundane uses as asking, "Please pass the salt." Or it can serve the exalted uses of praying to God and speaking about God. This commandment shows God's particular concern that we use our mouths to speak the truth about our neighbor.

My child

Giving false testimony usually results in someone's unfair punishment. Think about the years Joseph spent in prison because Potiphar's wife lied about him. Most of us have been put in a position where a teacher asks us to "tattle" on a classmate. Once our son's unwise teacher asked a whole group of guilty boys, simultaneously, to explain what had happened. Instead of comparing individual testimonies, he heard a fabricated story from one spokesman, which grew and was affirmed by all of the other listening hoodlums. Each had keeled in to peer pressure, knowing that to tell the truth would have endangered each and all of them. As a result, our son was unfairly disciplined. Those boys became more hardened and adept at lying. Deceit's power grows with peer practice.

What is the meaning of false testimony?

God knows all about these situations and gives us guidelines: if you are asked to testify, do it (Lev 5:1); don't just side with the majority or "join hands with a wicked man to be a malicious witness" (Exod 23:2–3); don't just side with a poor person because he is poor (Lev 19:15); don't just side with a great person because he is honored (Lev 19:15); the unanimous witness of two or more is to be counted as true (Deut 19:15); and maturity in Christ means not being carried along by "human cunning, by craftiness in deceitful schemes" (Eph 4:14).

A false testimony is particularly dangerous because it has the potential to kill, as when a generation of Israelites wandered forty years because ten men lied about the promised land. Or, remember the loathsome "witnesses" who brought about Naboth's death in the Bible. Naboth died because townsmen had been intimidated by Queen Jezebel into giving a false testimony. Therefore the punishment God prescribes fits the crime. "But as for . . . murderers, the sexually immoral, sorcerers, idolaters, and all liars, their portion will be in the lake that burns with fire and sulfur, which is the second death" (Rev 21:8).

My child

We don't need to be taught to lie. Lying comes naturally from our own sinful nature. Who has not heard their children, like mine, say, "He shoved me first."

"No, I didn't."

"Yes, you did."

Somebody has to be lying. One of them had to be bearing false testimony against the other. Which one? Just as the Bible says, "The one who states his case first seems right, until the other comes and examines him" (Prov 18:17).

Then there was the "Don't look at me; I didn't do it" faked innocence. In one sense, it was a relief when one son would be away, so the "not me" game couldn't be played successfully. As parents, we need the wisdom Solomon displayed with the two mothers. The Bible says "all men are liars," and my sons were out to prove the truth of God's word (Rom 3:4).

"Hurry! The bus will be here soon. Where is it? I know, today is library day. Where did you have it last? Did you check your backpack? Look under the couch." All of us began looking all over the house for my son's missing library book that was due back that day. I ended up writing a note to say we couldn't find it but would keep looking. However, after two fruitless weeks, we wrote a check for the cost of the book. About a year later, I moved the heavy dining room cupboard in order to clean. There was the book, slid way back underneath. I showed it to the boys, asking if either of them knew how it had gotten there. The culprit confessed that he had hidden the book ages ago because he felt his brother had been reading it instead of playing with him. "And you knew that he needed it, and would be fined for not returning it, yet you said nothing?"

The first lie came even before man sinned. Satan lied to Eve about the character and word of God. Satan "was a murderer from the beginning, and has nothing to do with the truth, because there is no truth in him. When he lies, he speaks out of his own character, for he is a liar, and the father of all lies" (John 8:44). How ironic that the liar accused God of lying! He even tried to twist God's word to God himself, tempting Jesus to jump from the temple. And later, he successfully incited false testimonies against Jesus, against God himself, before the Jewish council (Mark 14:56).

Lying and putting the blame on someone else is as old as time, literally. Adam blamed God, and he blamed Eve, who then blamed the serpent. Aaron blamed the Israelites (Exod 32:1–24). Saul blamed the people (1 Sam 15:1–23). Esau blamed his brother Jacob (Gen 27:36). And Pilate shifted blame to the crowd (Matt 27:24). What did they gain? What do you gain by lying, if you lose your soul?

Promises

Another form of lying is breaking a promise. If I give my word that I will do something, and then do not do it, I have lied. Elisabeth Elliot always advised people to do what they promised first, and then afterward duties and chores. In the Bible, one man's broken promise brought about his own death. Shimei had cursed David, revealing a lack of self-control and lack of respect for authority. So wise king Solomon made him promise that he would not leave town upon pain of death. Solomon knew the man would break his promise and so condemn himself. Similarly, God reserves severe punishments for liars: wealth is diminished (Prov 13:11), shame ensues (Prov 26:26), the mouth will be stopped (Ps 63:11), he won't escape (Prov 19:5), God's face is against him (1 Pet 3:10–12), he will not live out his days (Ps 55:23), he will be destroyed (Ps 5:6), he will not enter the holy city (Rev 21:27), he will go to hell (Rev 21:8).

When I was a single missionary, an American woman invited me multiple times to her home for lunch. When I finally accepted, I was treated as an inconvenience and an embarrassment. I never returned, and I never trusted her words again. I have to admit that I am thoroughly frustrated when someone lies because of cultural correctness. Some places in this world promote "politeness" in the form of lying and think this is acceptable. God wants our words to match our intent, our heart.

I'm sure I have often failed here as well. How many times have I promised someone that I would pray or phone or write? I scan their computer note, telling them I'll pray, and then click the next item, totally forgetting the promised intercession.

Slander

Slander also fits this category. A friend mentioned how one of the commentators on TV had seemed particularly mean-spirited. I suggested that the man was reacting just like a business man, only looking at the pragmatic angle. Did I know that? Could I see into his heart? I had spoken a testimony about the character of this man, who claimed to be a Christian. Had I spoken truly, or did I abuse him just because he was a dehumanized, distant, public figure? I don't think God cares how well we do or don't know someone as much as he cares about how truthful our tongue is. We can't slander anyone, even media stars.

It is so easy to slander, to charge someone with wickedness, isn't it? Yet God says that the one who lives on his holy hill "does not slander with his tongue and does no evil to his neighbor nor takes up a reproach against his friend" (Ps 15:3). He commands us: "You shall not go around as a slanderer among your people" (Lev 19:16). Even just listening to slander is evil: "An evildoer listens to wicked lips, and a liar gives ear to a mischievous tongue"(Prov 17:4).

The Ninth Commandment

God prescribes a more helpful alternative for dealing with wickedness in others. Instead of just talking about it, we are to go to the person, and confront him with his sin. If he doesn't repent, we take two or three others with us to confront him again. If he still doesn't repent, we take the matter to the church overseers (Matt 18:15–17).

My action

It is so easy to slander politicians, isn't it? Their every move seems so public. But what can I do with all the pent up frustration about their foolishness or immorality? Once God convicted me that instead of slandering the President, I should write a letter to him, confronting him about his personal, public sin. He probably never saw the letter, but God did. I probably should do that more often. I still really struggle here, as apparently most other people do as well, in a land where freedom of speech is so easy.

But what if the report about a person's deed is true, but maybe it's not a sin? "She really does dye her hair; you know I heard her say so herself." "He told me publicly that he has homosexual temptations." "Did you see what she had on in church! The way she dresses is something we ought to pray about for her." Now we cross into gossip, the tar pit for every woman. Entire magazines and TV shows devote themselves to gossip. God says that gossip is part of a reprobate mind and is encouraged by idleness (Rom 1:29; 1 Tim 5:13). Yet such behavior is almost an expected recreation among women, including Christian women. Whole churches have been split because of it. The Bible warns that a talebearer reveals secrets (Prov 11:13; 20:19); digs up evil (Prov 16:27); separates friends and sows strife (Prov 16:28; 17:9; 25:23).

My child

My children thought it was okay to mock teachers and report on classmates: "You know what she said and who got in trouble today!?" Their comments left a tainted picture of that student in my mind. But God's children should reject wives' tales (1 Tim 4:7), not associate with talebearers (Prov 20:19), faithfully conceal a matter (Prov 11:13), and bridle their own tongue (Jas 1:26). God wants us to build others up and "to speak evil of no one" (Titus 3:2). Isn't this the second great commandment: "Love your neighbor as yourself"? True love rejoices in the truth (1 Cor 13:6). If we knew love, then we would know how to love. "The one who loves knows better than anyone else how to conduct himself, how to serve the one he loves."[1] Consider how Joseph determined to quietly set Mary aside, rather than having her mocked and stoned.

I overheard a supposed friend make a biting remark about me. It hurt. All the sin in me wanted to vindicate myself, to put the other person down and hurt her the way she had hurt me. Elisabeth Elliot talks about such times as an opportunity to offer a sacrifice of ourselves; we sacrifice our rights to God. The Lord says, "Pray for those who persecute you" (Matt 5:44), and "Bless those who persecute you"(Rom 12:14). Often with tears from the battle within me and from the pain from without, I have knelt to pray. I didn't want to forgive. Who said obedience was easy? It is not easy. But it is necessary if I love my Lord. "Blessed are you when others revile you and persecute you and utter all kinds of evil against you falsely on my account. Rejoice and be glad, for your reward is great in heaven" (Matt 5:11–12). After more than forty years, I am still working on that last part.

Flattery

Lies can wear friendly smiles.
"That was the best sermon I have ever heard!"
"You should be heard internationally."
"When will you write a book on this?"
"You are so talented, so intelligent, so gifted."
"You look younger every time I see you!"

1. Elliot, *The Liberty of Obedience*. Also see Col 3:14, "Love covers a multitude of sins," and 1 Pet 4:8.

The Ninth Commandment

Flattery pleases men, not God (1 Thess 2:4-5). It fits right into his category of seven hated things. "Everyone utters lies to his neighbor; with flattering lips and with a double heart they speak. May the Lord cut off all flattering lips, the tongue that makes great boasts"(Ps 12:2-3). I once overheard my little son at a yard sale praise a toy someone was considering buying. He did it on purpose so that the customer might see my son's admiration for the object and leave it for him to have. We all do this in different ways. The Bible says that the sexually loose woman is particularly good at using her honeyed words, but her way leads to death (Prov 5:3; 7:5, 21). God warns us not to believe a flatterer because he is hiding wickedness in his heart (Ps 12:2; Prov 26:24-26). "His speech was smooth as butter, yet war was in his heart; his words were softer than oil, yet they were drawn swords" (Ps 55:21). Flattery sets a trap (Prov 29:5).

Think of all the ways in the Bible where flattery brought someone's downfall. Absalom flattered people at the gate and so turned their hearts away from his father, king David. Hushai flattered Absalom so that he chose the plan most harmful to himself. King Darius's advisors flattered him, thereby trapping him into signing an unjust law. Tertullus flattered Felix so as to prejudice him at Paul's trial. The Herodians flattered Jesus while trying to trap him into condemning himself. Judas's kiss of Christ hid treason.

Flattery given or received is a false testimony. When received, it deceives us into thinking more highly of ourselves than we ought (Rom 12:3; Gal 6:3). It distorts the truth, while tempting us to pride. Praise will test a man's true character (Prov 27:21) and can bring his ruin (Prov 26:28). I know a pastor who keeps a drawer full of critical letters as an antidote to the elixir of flattery. It is neither loving nor godly to flatter, because it subtracts from God's due praise. The psalmist exhorts: "I will bless the Lord at all times; his praise shall continually be in my mouth. My soul makes its boast in the Lord" (Ps 34:1-2). So we might more appropriately say to someone, "I praise God for his grace to me through you." The praise of God can never be falsely exaggerated.

My action

In contrast to the flatterer is the rebuker. Although it may seem counterintuitive, God says the rebuker finds more favor than a flatterer (Prov 28:23). Nathan rebuked David, which brought his repentance. Once our son asked for advice about a Christian who was sinning at school. After prayer, he confronted her with her sin, but she didn't repent. After more prayer, I went to her mother who was a dear friend, knowing I had to risk hurting her and our relationship. This was an incredibly painful and difficult conversation. I didn't want to do it. I was really scared. By God's grace, the mother right after hearing me quoted, "Faithful are the wounds of a friend" (Prov 27:6). Afterward, that godly mother confronted her daughter who then repented. Praise God, by his grace we are still friends.

Advertising

Other kinds of lying involve manipulation for selfish purposes or empty words. When I was in high school, I took a public speaking course. We were taught that in persuasive speech you must 1) create a need, 2) convince the person he must fulfill that need, and 3) persuade him that your idea best meets that need. Sound like the *modus operandi* of commercials? Advertising is mostly lies. "You are so great that you deserve this." "If you drink this, drive this, look like this, you will be popular, powerful, and pleased." Sound familiar? "Eat of our tree and you will be like God." The method uses lies. Flattery and exaggeration haven't changed since the Garden of Eden.

Can a Christian participate in false advertising? One of Pat Boone's Christian daughters recommended an acne treatment on TV. The problem was that she had never had skin problems. Like Joe Namath in pantyhose, celebrities often advertised things they didn't use. But because she was God's child, he would not let her get by with it. Legal briefs were filed, and she never starred in a TV commercial again as far as I know. For me, I would not have noticed or cared whether she had used the product, because the world's views have affected me so much.

Exaggeration

Exaggerations do not convey the truth either. "This is the best gift I ever got!" "My dog is the nicest anywhere." "I had the best seat ever!" "He is the meanest teacher in the world." When you stretch the facts, you often end up having to correct yourself, which God warns against. "Let not your mouth lead you into sin, and do not say before the messenger that it was a mistake. Why should God be angry at your voice and destroy the work of your hands?" (Eccl 5:6).

My child

When my sons were young, I got another one of those dreaded notes from the teacher. My son had exaggerated in a diet report, saying that he had eaten a half cup of vegetables for lunch, when the teacher could see very well that it was only a fourth cup.

So is a little enthusiasm wrong? What about in a job resumé or school application? For example, what if my resumé includes, "I led the ornithology club" (which consisted of I, myself, and me). God calls such talk "empty words." Exaggerations require you to sift through sentences to find the nuggets of fact. "Let no one deceive you with empty words, for because of these things the wrath of God comes upon the sons of disobedience" (Eph 5:6). Empty words seem to reproduce themselves like the useless brooms of the sorcerer's apprentice. "The words of a wise man's mouth win him favor, but the lips of a fool consume him. The beginning of the words of his mouth is foolishness, and the end of his talk is evil madness. A fool multiplies words, though no man knows what is to be, and who can tell him what will be after him?" (Eccl 10:12–14).

Testimony

Of course, the worst false witness I can give is to speak, or think, or live as if God were not true. "Who is the liar but he who denies that Jesus is the Christ"(1 John 2:22). Every time that I try in a conversation to ignore a distortion about who God is for the sake of peace, I have become an accomplice to a false testimony. Every time I shade what I speak about God or his word, I risk the charge of false testimony. That is one reason why the Bible says that teachers will be judged more harshly (Jas 3:1). Think about how angry God was with Job's friends because they did not speak what was right about God (Job. 42:7). What about my actions? Do I live as a practical atheist rather than as a Christian; that is, do I live according to my own wisdom without reference to God? If so, then I have lied about God to any observer present. I have suppressed the truth and exchanged the truth of God for a lie (Rom 1:18–23). Whenever I don't believe God, I have sided with Satan in calling God a liar. This is to join cosmic treason.

My testimony

"Don't you think that famous TV evangelist is wonderful?" a student asked. I knew the TV guy didn't have a clue about the true gospel, which included repentance from sin, and suffering for Christ, and self-denial. However, I wanted to witness to this wandering soul in a way that didn't call him a fool. Where to draw the line between a flat contradiction of his hero and passively ignoring false teaching for the sake of relationship? I ended up quoting some Scripture on suffering that we had covered in Bible study that day and saying that his hero didn't understand this. Did I obey the ninth commandment? I don't know.

Christ

The world rejects Christ. A couple years ago, my husband spoke to students at our house about the redemptive plot in *Pride and*

The Ninth Commandment

Prejudice. Mr. Darcy as the Christ figure comes to a lowly place where he is distrusted, slandered, gossiped about, disbelieved, scorned and publicly mocked, yet he never retaliates. Later he takes on his enemy and that of his bride, humbling himself for the sake of the loved one. That is a picture of Jesus. Christ was slandered as a Sabbath breaker, glutton, drunkard, and blasphemer. When he could have called legions of angels or struck people immediately with lightning, he chose to suffer quietly. All this persecution of one who never told a lie, "neither was deceit found in his mouth" (1 Pet 2:22; see Num 23:19; Heb 6:18).

Whatever he promised, he did, including giving himself to die. If he promises to give eternal life and a home in heaven to those who believe in him, you can be sure he will do it. Because he who promised is faithful, and all God's promises are fulfilled in him (2 Cor 1:20; Heb 10:23). Unlike us, he never flatters, exaggerates, says foolish empty words, or promises anything he won't do. The work of Christ is perfect.

Because the Son is the exact image of the Father, Jesus's revealing of that image of God is true. His testimony is true, both in word and life. Even the Father gives witness that the Son's imaging is true (John 5:36–37; 8:17–18). In fact, "Whoever does not honor the Son does not honor the Father who sent him" (John 5:23). Why? Because Jesus is God. He not only speaks truth, he is truth. "I am the way, and the truth, and the life" (John 14:6). Whatever is truth anywhere at any time found its origin in him. He is all truth. Only truth comes from his mouth (John 17:17; Titus 1:2). In fact, speech itself originates in him who is himself speech, the Word, the Logos. Christ as a true Son of his Father, who himself is the truth, gave true testimony to the glory of God both by his life and his word. The person of Christ is perfect.

My words pervert his truth and his glory. But Jesus's words are spotless, holy. "The words of the Lord are pure words, like silver refined in a furnace on the ground, purified seven times" (Ps 12:6). His righteousness, including his perfection in his speech, is counted as mine when I believe in Christ. All his goodness and perfect obedience (even in his talk) are imputed to me, considered to be mine. The Bible says all men are liars and that if any man does not sin with his mouth, he is perfect (Jas 3:2). Jesus as the God-man was and is perfect. "The Lord is our righteousness" (Jer 23:6). I have no goodness in myself. When I stand before the judgment throne, I am naked of anything to commend myself, unless Christ wraps his robe of righteousness around me. With the psalmist, I pray, "In you, O Lord, do I take refuge; let me never be put to shame; in Your righteousness deliver me!" (Ps 31:1). "May integrity and uprightness preserve me, for I wait for you" (Ps 25:21). This is not my uprightness, for I have none. This is Christ's uprightness, his righteousness, his goodness.

In the second part of *Pilgrim's Progress*, Mr. Great-heart describes Christ's righteousness. "Sin has delivered us up to the just curse of a righteous law . . . He ransomed you from your transgressions by blood, and covered your polluted and deformed souls with righteousness."[2] Bunyan refers to Jesus's teaching that says that if a man has two coats and sees someone in need, he must give away one. He applies this to us. "Now, our Lord indeed hath two coats [of righteousness], one for himself, and one to spare; wherefore he freely bestows one upon those that have none. And thus, Christiana and Mercy, and the rest of you that are here, doth your pardon come by deed, or by the work of another Man. Your Lord Christ is he that worked, and hath given away what he wrought for, to the next poor beggar he meets [us]."[3] "And by this righteousness, and no other, they are fully justified from all condemnation in the sight of God. Of this righteousness, therefore, they glory, and their souls make their boast of it . . . [For it] is of the essence of the gospel, enters into the life and joy of faith, brings relief to the conscience, and influences to the love of the Lord our righteousness, and to bring forth the fruits of righteousness, which are by him to the praise and glory of God."[4] "So by the one man's obedience the many will be made righteous" (Rom 5:19).

2. Bunyan, *The Pilgrims Progress*, 375.
3. Ibid.
4. Ibid., 374, footnote by Rev. Joseph Ivimey.

The Ninth Commandment

Response

But not only does he dress us in his righteousness, including a belt of truth, he activates actual righteousness in us through the Holy Spirit. The Holy Spirit himself is the Spirit of truth (1 John 5:6). We are born again. I have a new heart that loves God. God's Spirit lives in us. We can now do what is pleasing to him. We can shut our mouths instead of lying or slandering (Ps 34:13; Prov 10:19; Eph 4:25, 31–32; Col 3:8-10). God will set a guard over the door of our mouths (Ps 141:3). We can repent and receive the mercy of forgiveness and cleanness (Prov 28:13; Jas 5:16; 1 John 1:9). We can speak the truth to others in love. With a new heart, we can speak out of the overflow of that new heart what reflects the glory of our Father (Matt 12:35–37). "He put a new song in my mouth, a song of praise to our God. Many will see and fear, and put their trust in the Lord" (Ps 40:3). "I will bless the Lord at all times; his praise shall continually be in my mouth" (Ps 34:1–2; see Ps 12:6; 51:15; 71:15, 17; Heb 13:15). Not only are we made righteous in our hearts and mouths, but also he promises us blessings for telling the truth, including long life and seeing good days (Deut 25:15; 1 Pet 3:10), living in God's holy hill (Ps 15:1–2; 24:3–4), receiving God's delight and establishment (Prov 12:19,22), being a delight of kings (Prov 16:13), being favored and highly esteemed before God and man (Prov 3:3–4), receiving mercy (Prov 28:13), and inheriting God's promised land (Deut 16:20). Who would exchange these gifts for a lie?

We know a man who survived Auschwitz only to live under the tyranny of Nicolae Ceausescu in Romania. Because the man had a doctorate in economics, he was called upon to give financial reports and projections to the government. He knew the truth of the communist decrepit results and told the truth. Although the government falsified his reports, he continued to be consulted. Prov 16:13 tells us that truth tellers are valued by kings, evidently even bad ones. Wise men keep liars far from them (Prov 30:6). As

Elisabeth Elliot notes, "The man whose eye is single for the glory of Another can be trusted."[5]

Here is the true witness that God gives and that he expects us to give. The Son of God, Lord of the universe, came into this world to save sinners, of which I am one. If we give a true witness, God will use our witness to deliver souls (Ps 40:3; Prov 14:25). The lie of Satan will be undone, since Christ reverses the curse. We can imitate God and be his coworker in truth. After all, God gave men to be pastors and teachers, truth tellers. "You are my witnesses," Jesus said (Matt 28:19-20; Act 1:8). Our new mouth undoes sin and glorifies God to the praise of Christ. Eventually God will receive a true testimony about his glory, both from his children and from the world, for "at the name of Jesus every knee should bow, in heaven and on earth and under the earth, and every tongue confess that Jesus Christ is Lord, to the glory of God the Father" (Phil 2:10-11). Even all creation will sing of his praises: "The heavens declare the glory of God, and the sky above proclaims his handiwork. Day to day pours out speech" (Ps 19:1-2).

In the meantime, I fight my desire to please men by shading the truth. Do I tell her how awful the painting is and how I hate the way it distorts what God made? Do I comfort her by excusing her son's sin as if it were so common as to be acceptable? Do I keep my mouth shut when she vaunts herself with another highly generalized opinion? Does truth demand that I tell my son I am not happy about his staying up late to watch the game? Again I sit and cry, "Father make me righteous; make my mouth praise You." And in all this we are more than conquerors through Christ Jesus who loved us and fulfilled the righteous requirement of the law out of that love for us (Rom 8:4, 37).

---

5. Elliot, *Discipline*, 70.

10

The Tenth Commandment

Jesus Reconciles

> You shall not covet your neighbor's house; you shall not covet your neighbor's wife, or his male servant, or his female servant, or his ox, or his donkey, or anything that is your neighbor's. (Exod 20:17)

My child

"Please, Mommy! I promise if you get me the GI Joe Headquarters, I'll never ask for anything else the rest of my life."

His sweet face looked pleadingly at me, enough to break my mother's heart. Yet I knew that what he wanted would be extravagant. How I longed to give him the world, not just a tower of plastic. I would have thrown myself in front of a raging bull if it would have saved his life. Would my giving in to his desire confirm that to him? Would he understand that the toy was a mere symbol of an effusive, sacrificial love? Or, would he just be content with the thing in itself? Or worse, would it be just one more thing to desire, grow tired of, and later lead to hungering for a greater "thing"? My husband and I decided to splurge, not only out of a love for him, but also to teach him a lesson. In later years when he requested something, we often quoted his hollow words back to him, "If I had this, I would never ask for anything else the rest of my life."

The whole idea of coveting doesn't even seem like sin in today's culture. In fact, it is the expected norm of materialism. Our culture tells us we can have everything and anything now, without even paying—just use credit. I will never forget the beauty of a pearl drifting luxuriously down through a bottle of Prell shampoo in a TV commercial. Don't you want it? Of course you do, and you can have it now. The entire marketing industry is based on the premise that people are selfish, envious, and greedy. But God says coveting is not even to be mentioned as a fault among Christians (Eph 5:3).

What does it mean to covet?

Coveting takes on so many characteristics. But for the sake of clarity, I have broken it into four nuances. (1) Sticking close to the commandment's own wording, "covet" means wanting something that belongs to someone else, or an inordinate desire. (2) Envy, which emphasizes wanting something similar to what belongs to someone else. In contrast to coveting, it excludes any idea of taking it away from them. (3) Complaining, which centers on wanting something more or something different from what I now have. This does not have to involve another person at all. (4) Ingratitude, which focuses on liking what I have, but assuming I deserve it.

My child

While we visited with a married couple, our sons played with their dog. When we had to leave, tears rolled down the boys' cheeks: "Can't we take Lassie home with us?"

"Maybe when you are older we can have our own dog."

"But we want Lassie."

It wasn't just any dog that they wanted. It was this large, gentle one with the beautiful coat of warm fur that belonged to our friends.

King Ahab looked from his palace window at Naboth's fruitful vineyard and coveted what did not belong to him. King David looked from his palace roof at the beautiful wife of Uriah and coveted what did not belong to him. Eli's sons coveted sacrifices belonging to God. All of these people held positions of authority. Power adds a different dimension of possibility to coveting. Tyranny can demand by force what does not belong to it. But this sin is no respecter of social station. The soldier, Achan, coveted silver belonging to God. The servant Gehazi coveted the clothes offered as a reward to Elijah. Both connived to get what they wanted. Balaam wanted reward money that God had denied him (Num 22 and 2 Pet 2:15). Judas coveted the money that belonged to the disciples (John 12:6). Eve wanted the fruit that belonged to God.

God warns us to beware of coveting, even to flee from it (1 Tim 6:10-11). Why? Because it brings no satisfaction (Hag 1:6); troubles our home (Prov 15:27); causes us to stray from the faith; saddens us (1 Tim 6:10); causes our possessions to be given to others (Jer 6:13, 8:10); breaks fellowship with Christians (1 Cor 5:11); calls down on us the wrath of God (Col 3:5-6); and prevents us from inheriting the kingdom (Eph 5:5). God hates coveting, considers it idolatry, and rejects any man from ministry who regularly engages in it (Ps 10:3; Col 3:5; 1 Tim 3:3; Titus 1:7).

With such dire results, we might be concerned about liking anything in this world at all. So where is the line between freely enjoying what God gives and sinfully coveting? Ezekiel guides us here. "For with lustful talk in their mouths they act; their heart is set on their gain" (Ezek 33:31). The condemnation comes for how their hearts are set, for how they want the gift more than God the giver.

My actions

As a preteen, I wanted silky skin promised by an expensive lotion. When I came home with it, my parents immediately walked me back to the store to return it. I got a lecture about the frivolousness of outward beauty and the deviousness of marketing.

We can understand the difference between coveting and simple appreciation of something by looking at another family interaction. When as a teenager my father gave me a stereo, the gift was exciting, overwhelming! But deep inside I knew that the gift only showed more intensely my father's love. I would have exchanged that stereo in a moment, if it would have saved my father's life. The key is the heart.

Does our heart love God more than these? Jesus says, "Where your treasure is there your heart will be also" (Matt 6:21). It's not a matter of wearing one threadbare outfit the rest of your life in order to try to punish or deny your desires. (I attempted this as a young Christian.) Such behavior doesn't change the heart. Hermits in caves still dream of women. It is a matter of sanctification where we love God most, where the heart has been made new (Mark 7:21–23).

Coveting wants the creation more than the Creator and exchanges one for the other on the pedestal of the heart. "If anyone loves the world, the love of the Father is not in him. For all that is in the world—the desires of the flesh and the desires of the eyes and pride in possessions—is not from the Father but is from the world. And the world is passing away along with its desires, but whoever does the will of God abides forever" (1 John 2:15–17). This is the one commandment Paul struggled with (Rom 7:7-8). Why? Because it was not just a matter of outward self-control. It had to do with the very center of his being, of what he thought and who he was. The fact that God judges coveting shows his ability to see into our hearts; it shows his concern with the purity of our hearts. "Man looks on the outward appearance but the Lord looks on the heart" (1 Sam 16:7).

Unseen things can be coveted as much as seen things—things such as love, health and life. I would have given almost anything to obtain healing for my father in his last illness. Life does not have a money value. Relationships and love are priceless. If my son gave me an expensive gift but never came to see me, which would be more important? If your child voluntarily helped around the

The Tenth Commandment

house, or if he accepted your advice about life decisions, which action would you treasure more? Life itself can be our greatest temptation. Once we prayed with parents who struggled with the knowledge that their child would get a heart transplant and maybe live, if another parent's child died. How painfully they released their child to God's will, confessing they coveted their neighbor's life for the sake of their own child's life.

Everything is lent to us by God, including our children, our talents, our own breath, all that is seen and unseen. "What do you have that you were not given?" (1 Cor 4:7). Am I willing to lay down those things—his things—as sacrifices on the altar if God asks for them? Do I cling to them, saying, "No, I want this. You can't have it." Here Jesus warns us: "What does it profit a man to gain the whole world and forfeit his soul?" (Mark 8:36). "If anyone would come after me, let he deny himself and take up his cross and follow me" (Matt 16:24). It is not a matter of never enjoying a toy, a relationship, a job, or excellence in a performance. It is a matter of loving God more and loving my neighbor more. When we love others, we want what is best for them, even if it means our own loss. When we love God most, looking into Christ's face on the cross and his sacrifice for us, all our treasures become expendable.

My husband tells me that when he used to bike near his college, he would pass beautiful mansions. Instead of wishing he could live there, he began praying. "God, that one is especially nice. Would you give me one like that in heaven?" I tried to do this. So when I saw a lady in church with a gorgeous sweater and another with thick, wavy hair, I prayed God would likewise bless me in heaven.

Envy

I look at what other people have, and I want it. Sometimes it's a house or piece of clothing. Usually it's an intangible. Other descendants of Adam and Eve, besides me, have repeated similar sins. Cain envied God's approval of his brother's sacrifice. The Philistines desired Isaac's property (Gen 26:13–21). Laban's sons envied Jacob's growing herds (Gen 31). Shechem's son envied Jacob's riches. Rachel wanted to have children like her sister, who in turn wanted her husband's favor. Joseph's brothers envied their father's affections for his younger son. Miriam, Aaron, and Korah envied Moses's position (Num 16:3; Ps 106:16–18). Saul envied the praise given to David after a victorious battle. King Uzziah desired the priests' ability to offer incense in the temple. Haman couldn't bear the honor given to Mordecai (Esth 6:6–12). King Nebuchadnezzar's advisors envied Daniel's prestige. Sanballat and Tobiah did not want anyone seeking the good of the Israelites (Neh 2:10). In the parable of the prodigal son, the elder brother envied the lavish attention given the younger brother. The all-day workers in the parable chafed at their employer's generosity toward later workers. The temple priests envied Jesus (Matt 27:11–18). Such envy brings strife, confusion, evil work (Jas 3:14, 16), backbiting (2 Cor 12:20), and rots the bones (Prov 14:30).

My attitude

In my single years, I tried to read a book written to a girl who was about to marry a young man I had liked. Why her? Why not me? I could be a good wife, maybe even a better one for him. I threw the book down in disgust and envy. God tells us not to begrudge someone else their blessings (Jas 5:9). Or in a later instance, I asked, "Why did she just pop out healthy babies in a few minutes and I nearly died in childbirth?" God tells me that if I really loved her, I wouldn't envy her but would be happy for her.

Love does not envy (1 Cor 13:4). Love rejoices with those who rejoice (Rom 12:15). Love seeks the good of the other person (1 Cor 10:24). Sometimes my envy is for my husband. I want the world to honor him and see what a great and godly man he is. When someone else's book gets front page advertisement, or recommended on the internet instead of his, I disobey Gal 5:26: "Let us not become conceited, provoking one another, envying one another." This attitude inhibits my own spiritual growth, although I am loathe to admit it (1 Pet 2:1–2). God hates envy and will repay us for it (Ezek 35:11). As the sovereign God, he is free to do as he wishes with what belongs to him, including honors (Matt 20:15).

I can usually rationalize feelings of envy under the heading of "justice according to me." I'm sure Eve did this as well. I can hear her thoughts as they echo in her descendant, me. "God is great and knows everything. Why can't I know everything, too? If this tree would do it for me, why would he keep it from me? Doesn't he love me? Obviously, the serpent understands things about God's ways that he has not revealed to me. I want to be like that, too. I want to know what God knows. I want his wisdom. I want to be God."

My child

The Bible says, "You covet and cannot obtain, so you fight and quarrel" (Jas 4:2). Sometimes coveting the honor of being better than someone else is the problem. Are boys competitive? Is the sky blue? Each of our sons envied the accomplishments of the other, sometimes trying harder to compete, or sometimes giving up in dismay. When one son received an award, the other whispered to me that he could never accomplish that. Even though I encouraged him that he didn't know what God would do with him, his face fell. Each tried to outdo the other in soccer, acting, band performances, solos, whatever they put their hand to. When one performed a long famous poem for a class presentation, the other picked up the poetry book and started memorizing an even longer poem. When one got a remote control car, the other boy had to race it in a shorter time; then the first boy had to take a curve faster; then the other boy had to figure how to do a jump; then the first boy had to get it to flip. The never ending escalation of competition, growing out of envy, overrides so many boyish decisions. I never knew how blessed I was to have a sister.

My attitude

Envy does not necessarily mean wanting to take away something from another person or even hating the fact that someone else has something I don't. It can just mean we wish we had the same thing. When in high school Linda Johnson got to sing a solo, I didn't want her to lose that privilege. It was just that I wanted to have a solo, too.

When I was in seminary, living in the women's dorm, I thought about how each girl had qualities that I wished I had. One sensitively knew how to encourage each burdened heart. Another confidently steamed through every situation in faith. A beautiful, intelligent girl who had been a model often unintentionally made me ashamed of my dumpy build. A roommate seemed to know everything about God, the Bible, famous Christians, and how to apply all that to life. Another roommate delighted in spending hours alone with God. One girl had a tremendous testimony of coming out of the darkness of sin. Some got engaged.

I wanted what each of them had. Elisabeth Elliot counsels, "But the question to precede all others, which finally determines the course of our lives is 'What do I really want?' Was it to love what God commands . . . and to desire what He promises? Did I want what I wanted, or did I want what He wanted, no matter what it might cost?"[1]

There will come a time when all Christians will be envied—the last day. God tells us that the wicked will see Christians exalted with honor and that this will grieve and anger them (Ps 112:9–10). No one has ever seen, nor can even imagine, the wonders God has prepared for those who love him (1 Cor 2:9). At God's right hand there are pleasures forever (Ps 16:11). We should be comforted knowing that although God is generous toward the wicked now, this life is the closest thing to heaven they will ever know. After all, we deserve hell as much as they do. So he counsels us not to envy the wicked (Ps 37:1; Prov 3:31; 23:17; 24:1, 19).

---

1. Elliot, *Passion and Purity*, http://www.goodreads.com/quotes/266921-but-the-question-to-precede-all-others-which-finally-determines.

How encouraging to see in the Bible that Jonathan rejoiced with David and wanted him to have everything, including his own crown (1 Sam 18:1-4; 19:1-7; 20:1-43; 23:16-18). Then later John the Baptist appeared with his famous phrase, "He must increase and I must decrease" (Matt 3:11-13, Mark 1:7-8, John 3:26-31).

What a wonderful freedom would break over my soul if I could say that with all my heart! I need to fellowship more with people like that. Perhaps you do, too. In fact, God warns us to stay away from envious people (1 Tim 6:4-5). People who envy walk in the flesh, not the Spirit (1 Cor 3:3). Love overturns this sin. If I follow the second great commandment to love my neighbor as myself, I will never envy. I need to claim God's mercy toward me in Christ and trust his word that "those who seek God don't lack" (Ps 34:10). I pray with the psalmist, "Lord incline my heart to your testimonies and not to envy" (Ps 119:36).

Complaining

Coveting also involves complaining, wanting more things or different things. King David, who already had several wives, coveted Bathsheba who belonged to someone else. He was not content with beautiful, intelligent Abigail or any of the other seven wives. Martha, not content with Jesus's presence, appealed to Jesus to make her sister help her with preparing the meal. John D. Rockefeller when asked by a reporter how much money was enough, answered, "Just a little bit more." Single women want to be married. Married women want different husbands. Everyone wants a different body. But "to love God is to love His will. It is to wait quietly for life to be measured by One who knows us through and through. It is to be content with His timing and His wise appointment."[2] This includes his choice of discipline and "polishing" through hardship.

---

2. Elliot, http://www.goodreads.com/quotes/355291-to-love-god-is-to-love-his-will-it-is.

My Child, His Child

My child

Because of God's commandment, "Do everything without arguing or questioning" (Phil 2:14), we had a rule in our home that complaining would have consequences. Whatever you complained about got doubled. When one son fussed about making his bed, he had to do it twice. When the other argued about taking out the garbage cans, he had to do it twice. Once I brought home a coconut so the boys could see what it looked like, how to open it, and how it had milk inside. We tasted some of the raw coconut for dinner that night. One son got four helpings before he stopped protesting.

The Israelites had manna in the wilderness, and in fact goat's milk and lamb, but they complained as if they had nothing because they longed for the fish, onions, garlic and meat of Egypt. "So he gave them their request, but sent a wasting disease among them" (Ps 106:15). Because of their grumbling at least ten times, God said he was angry enough to kill them all instantly. Just this one generation experienced outbreaks of plagues, snake attacks, and explosions of fire as a result of their complaining. God might give us our desire, but also give us a "lean soul," an estrangement from him (Ps 106:14–15). We have bent our wills toward desire, but not desire for God (Ps 119:36–37). We don't have what we want because we don't ask God for it, and he sometimes doesn't give it because all we want to do is use it for ourselves, not for his glory (Jas 4:3).

What happens when we get what we ask for? I'll never forget a poster outside of a church. You could just see the top of a man's hair above the sea. Both of his hands were clenched above the water with fistfuls of dollars. He had what he wanted but was drowning (Eccl 4:6). Even the seemingly good desires we have may not be good in God's sight. If Hezekiah had not been granted his request for extended life, Manasseh would not have been born, perpetrating a bloody reign of terror. Rachel wanted children but died in childbirth. Did you ever pray for children, and then say to God, "But did it have to be these?" Did you ever have one of those days where you wished you had never had children? "Where is the blessing, God? All I'm getting is stabbed in the back and a lot of pain. I must be a total failure to have such rotten kids." God had children, too, who stabbed him in the side, the hands, and the feet. I was one of those children.

My attitude

After college, I worked as a gopher at a Christian conference. (You know: go for this; go for that; go for whatever is needed.) I was complaining to God as I stapled news sheets together that I could have been listening to Francis Schaeffer in that room over there. Then I heard someone approach my desk and ask for help. I looked up into the eyes of Corrie Ten Boom. If I had not been at that desk at that moment I would never have had the privilege of meeting and escorting her to the lobby. I made a mental note to myself to never complain again because God obviously knew better than I did. That resolution probably lasted less than twenty-four hours.

Eve wasn't satisfied with the Garden of Eden. Although she had a perfect husband, perfect body, perfect soul, perfect relation with God, perfect relation with her husband and all creation, all the food she wanted, friendly animals, perfect weather, gorgeous flowers and trees, she had to have more. Now all of creation groans or complains under the weight of sin that Eve and Adam brought. If only she had been content with perfection. But God tells us that the eyes and ears are never satisfied (Eccl 1:8). "The willingness to be and to have just what God wants us to be and have, nothing more, nothing less, and nothing else, would set our hearts at rest, and we would discover the simpler life, the greater peace."[3]

But we don't have perfection, so we think that gives us an excuse to be discontent. We might whine, which is just another form of complaining based ultimately on coveting our own way. God told Paul who didn't want his thorny affliction, "My grace is sufficient for you" (2 Cor 12:9). If we could be content along with being godly, unlike Eve, we would gain all happiness (1 Tim 6:6–8; Heb 13:5).

3. Elisabeth Elliot, http://www.goodreads.com/quotes/379879-the-willingness-to-be-and-to-have-just-what-god.

My attitude

Nothing brought more discontented greed to my heart than when the *Sears Wish Book* arrived each year before Christmas. I went through every page of the toyland extravaganza. Whenever I saw what I wanted, I circled the item number. If I really, really wanted it, it got several circles. I must have circled every doll outfit for my Betsy McCall doll. When I didn't get every one of them, I tried to sew together cloth scraps to make up what was missing.

Discontentment leads to greedy self-appeasement. I get whatever I want, because I am worth it, because I want it. We have forgotten to buy according to our needs, rather than our wants. But the two get confused when clever advertising promotes a luxury item as a "need." God has promised to provide all our needs according to his riches in glory in Christ Jesus (Phil 4:19). Do I believe that? Do I rationalize that since he wants me to be happy and since he gave me all these goods and opportunities, I should avail myself of them? I have forgotten that all goods belong to God. I have forgotten to ask if there were a better way to use the resource of a paycheck to bring him more glory. Have you ever struggled with this?

My child

I don't know what was the worst, the grocery store, or the toy store, or later the sports store. Every time I took one of my sons to these places there would be at least three things or more in our cart that were not originally considered to be needed. Internet does not have the same appeal as going to a store and actually putting your hands on something and putting it in your take home bag. These trips always squeezed me into making quick decisions about money, material quality, generosity versus thrift lessons, and what is love in this situation. It didn't help when they would add, "That brand of cleat shoes is the healthiest for your feet."

My attitude

Personally, I used to hate going to the mall because every window display, color arrangement, and entrance item was intended to cause me to covet, to make me dissatisfied with what I had and to desire more. I would come home looking at my drab house with piles of papers and books. Then slowly God changed my view. Instead of coveting the beautiful things for myself, I tried just admiring the beauty, creativity and craftsmanship God had given among men. That would include merchandise owned by a shop proprietor. His desire for me to covet his merchandise still does not make it right for me to covet, to be discontent with what God has given me.

It didn't always counter my lusts. Why can't I be satisfied? Billy Graham with a nod to Augustine offers, "God made us with this huge capacity and desire in order that he might come in and completely satisfy that desire. God made the human heart so big that only he can fill it. He made it demand so much that only he can supply that demand."[4]

Perhaps it's not so much a thing that makes us discontent as it is a situation, a very difficult and painful situation. Spurgeon compares this to being a lighthouse. Lighthouses are of necessity often built on precarious promontories. Their value proves itself in the storm, but not in the stillness; they are valued in the darkness, but not in the daylight. "So with the Spirit's work: if it were not on many occasions surrounded with tempestuous waters, we should not know that it was true and strong: if the winds did not blow upon it, we should not know how firm and secure it was. The master-works of God are those men who stand in the midst of difficulties, stedfast [sic], unmoveable.[sic] . . . He who would glorify God must set his account upon meeting with many trials."[5]

---

4. Billy Graham, *Decision* (July-August, 2011), 4.
5. Spurgeon, *Morning and Evening*, 128.

Ingratitude

Complaining is just the verbalization or attitude of discontent in the heart. The underlying attitude is "God doesn't know what he is doing. I know better than he does." This is a form of unbelief. Grumbling means to love oneself to the point of being unthankful (2 Tim 3:2), to run down the lane where our lusts and self-centeredness are hiding (Jude 16), to thirst for our own luxurious possessions. We don't remember God's mercies and the fact that we deserve nothing but hell (Ps 106:7; Isa 1:2–3; Jer 2:5–6; Hos 13:6). We ultimately say with Eve, "God, you are not enough"; "Your gifts are paltry." Yet he has given us exceeding abundantly above all that we ask or think.

My child

Several months after high school graduation, one son bitterly exploded that we had not given him a car, which many of his friends had received as a graduation gift. But we had offered to pay half of his college tuition, buy his dorm furniture, fly him to appointments, help him find a good roommate, church, and Christian college group. We would help him find research material and study for exams. But somehow that wasn't enough.

We are made heirs of all things, seated on thrones with him, crowned with life, given everlasting waters, eternal life, appointed judges of angels, cleansed, forgiven, clothed in white robes of righteousness, redeemed, released from the bondage of sin, its power, and its guilt, granted power to believe, called children of God, given his Spirit to overcome the world, the flesh, and the devil, healed of our diseases, given gifts and the fruit of the Holy Spirit, will be confessed before angels, inscribed with the name of God, will be made a pillar in the temple of God, and feast at his table with him. He has promised to never leave us or forsake us, to give us wisdom when we ask and guide us through life. Jesus who is heir of all things has made us co-heirs with him through his crucifixion and resurrection. Is this not enough? Must I still covet that latest trinket that will be despised in a decade?

My attitude

When I was twelve years old, my seven year old sister gave me a gift of Molly and Polly paper dolls. In my disappointment, I blurted out that I was too old for paper dolls. I'm sure I hurt my sister. Little did I know the hours that the two of us would spend together in imaginary places with those dolls. I still have them and wish I still had her to play with. A thorn pierces me to this day when I consider my ingratitude.

Even owning a relationship is a gift from God. Being a grateful steward of the gift of a friend is the opposite of coveting relationships. Being grateful makes the heart merry (Prov 15:13,15). "Well, it rained on the picnic—but thankfully it didn't snow!" Paul knew this secret of contentment (Phil 4:12–13). Gratitude, which engenders humility, cuts off coveting. So when grateful contentment is the escort of godliness, we gain much spiritually (1 Tim 6:6). Part of the cure for covetousness is thankful praying (Eph 5:19-20; Col 4:2; 1 Thess 5:17-18).

The book and movie *Pollyanna* has an orphaned missionary child who teaches others the "glad game." In essence, it was a way to see the silver lining in every rain cloud. So when she remembers a walking cane coming in a care package, the family played the game by thinking how glad they were that they didn't have to use the cane. The memory of this story always convicts me.

Another cure for coveting is glad surrender to God. "Whatever you want, Lord, whatever you choose. Not my will but thine be done." "It is in our acceptance of what is given that God gives Himself."[6] Not to covet the fulfillment of our own will underlies this commandment, not to imitate Eve's desire to be like God in deciding what is right and good.

---

6. Elliot, *These Strange Ashes*, http://www.goodreads.com/quotes/255853-it-is-in-our-acceptance-of-what-is-given-that.

My attitude

I hear myself pray, "If my son doesn't return safely from his skiing trip, you know best." But then I struggle and plead and sometimes fight with God for what I think is best. Nevertheless, the final outcome is always the same by way of necessity more than sanctification: "Your will be done."

Christ

In fact, it is not simply a problem that I covet more and want it on my own terms. But I can't pay for what I have. I actually owe for everything, including my very life. This is an impossible charge on my bill. But Christ paid the debt we owed to God. We owed him our death as payment for sin—"the soul who sins shall die" (Ezek 18:4). We had earned our own death by doing the work of sin. "The wages of sin is death" (Rom 6:23). I owed God my eternal death because I had rebelled against an eternally holy God when I broke his commands. Nothing else could be used as payment. If I gained the whole world for my ransom, would I be giving to him anything more than what he already owned? My blood was the only proper payment for sin. I owed it. Yet Jesus came and paid my bill. He signed the check with his blood. Everything I owed, he paid.

Christ as God's true child, only Son, did not sin, and therefore did not covet. "Jesus loved the will of His Father. He embraced the limitations, the necessities, the conditions, the very chains of His humanity as He walked and worked here on earth, fulfilling moment by moment His divine commission and the stern demands of His incarnation. Never was there a word or even a look of complaint."[7]

He must have been content being single, never having a family or children, not having brothers and sisters who supported him, working at a trade in a small town, getting tired, never having a home, being hated by authorities and synagogue members, not

---

7. Elliot, http://www.goodreads.com/quotes/355292-jesus-loved-the-will-of-his-father-he-embraced-the.

owning a closetful of clothes, not traveling around the world, not being handsome, not owning a donkey for transport, not owning land or a company, not living with the privileged riches of the wealthy, not even having any food sometimes, not being appointed as a professor at an academy, not winning an election, not publishing a single word in his earthly lifetime, not earning a degree or graduating from an institution, not being duly crowned king of kings or proclaimed high priest, or grabbing his attributes as God (Phil 2). All of these must have been faced as temptations to covet, and yet he despised them. The Bible says, "He endured the cross, despising the shame," for the joy set before him (Heb 12:2).

He knew that all things were his. "All things that are mine are yours, and yours are mine" (John 17:10). But that "all" was fulfilled through knowing and being known by his Father. "In Your presence is fullness of joy." He was completely content in trinitarian love before the earth was ever made. This is the epitome of completion. We can be content as well in that everlasting love, which is what Jim Elliot meant when he said, "He is no fool who gives what he cannot keep to gain that which he cannot lose."[8]

Coveting is the one command that no one, not even the legalist, can hide from. All stand guilty before the bar of God. No one can say he has kept the Ten Commandments when he sees this heart requirement. The law shines a light to show the debris in each of us (Rom 7). But just seeing the problem does not cure the problem. My savior brings that. He comes with the comfort of his death, in which the sinful me also died (Rom 6:1–2). He comes with his resurrection, in which I receive newness of life. I know that he lives to always intercede in prayer for me and that the good work that he began in me he will complete. I am free because I have been forgiven. I am free to love him back and to give up my insistence today on a model body, an exemplary house, perfect children, retrieval of lost relationships, guilt over things undone, guilt over things done, jealousies, egotistical goals. I can

---

8. Elliot, *Journals of Jim Elliot*, October 28, 1949, journal entry, 174. Quoted in Justin Taylor, "He Was No Fool," https://blogs.thegospelcoalition.org/justintaylor/2010/01/08/he-ws-no-fool/.

find sufficient love in my Father because his love draws me into his unfathomable riches of himself and out of the tawdry world.

Response

God tells us to put away envy (1 Pet 2:1) and to mortify covetousness, which is idolatry (Rom 13:9; Col 3:5). How in the world can I do this? Maybe that means slipping into the wastebasket those beautiful magazine pictures, or going to the mall with credit cards left at home, or sticking to a list of gifts prayed over ahead of time, or simply saying "no" in denial to myself. If this were my last day on earth, what would God have me do with my desires and resources so as to bring him glory? Would I sell it all in order to obtain the pearl of great price, which is Christ and his blessings? "Seek first the kingdom of God and his righteousness and all these things shall be added to you" (Matt. 6:33). "Give me neither poverty nor riches and feed me with allotted food" (Prov 30:8). Blessed are you if you hate coveting, then your days will be long (Prov 28:16). A man's life does not consist in things (Luke 12:15). Incline my heart to your testimonies, not covetousness (Ps 119:36). The cure is prayer (Col 3). Be a shining light (Phil 2:14–15).

Here is the trash can into which we can pitch our envy, jealousy, greed, self-aggrandizement, and pride. As Paul says, "I count them but rubbish in order that I may gain Christ" (Phil 3:8). All the things, relationships, and gifts of this world are less than a shadow in the presence of our glorious God. To be so honored to call him Lord and Father, to be known by him is the greatest blessing. It is the heart of his covenant, "I will be your God and you will be my people." "For what will it profit a man if he gains the whole world and forfeits his soul?" (Matt 16:26). Nothing compares to knowing and being known in love by God. Paul surely understood that this God could be trusted to supply all his needs, and mine.

The earthly cannot supplant the heavenly. Accumulation of materials or even "friends" does not fill the heart, nor does the quest for meaning under the sun, nor does the desire to live. Even the closest of relationships, as between a mother and her child, disintegrate and disappoint, leaving a mother abandoned and feeling futile. If your treasure is in your child, or any other place apart from God, you will be crushed. God warns,"For where your treasure is, there your heart will be heart also" (Matt 6:21).

We can't make our children repent. We can intercede for them asking God to grant them repentance, and we can ask that they not be led into temptation but delivered from evil. One of my prayers for my children, when they persisted in making foolish decisions in the area of relationships, was that God would hedge up their ways. "Therefore, behold I will hedge up your way with thorns, and make a wall, that she shall not find her paths. And she shall follow after her lovers, but she shall not overtake them; and she shall seek them, but shall not find them: then shall she say, I will go and return to my first husband; for then was it better with me than now " (Hos 2:6–7). We need that hedge, too.

How does our focus change? "One does not surrender a life in an instant, that which is lifelong can only be surrendered in a lifetime."[9] We can always begin with repentance. I have forgiveness through repentance, which is another gift (Acts 11:18; 2 Tim 2:25). When I look at all my sins I can get really discouraged. How can I ever do what is pleasing to God? "Then you will remember your own evil ways, and your doings that were not good, and shall loathe yourselves in your own sight for your iniquities and for your abominations" (Ezek 36:31). Someone pointed out to me once that the longer we live as Christians, the more wicked we see ourselves to be. This is not because we are becoming more wicked. On the contrary, we are becoming more sanctified and that very sanctification shines an increasingly bright light on our sins that were hidden and on the pure holiness of Christ. We hate sin more and love Jesus more. I realize that I can never fulfill God's standards of perfection, nor can I even repent properly. But Christ is at work within me both to will and to do his good pleasure. He accepts me and gives me grace to repent and be forgiven.

---

9. Elliot, *Shadow of the Almighty*, http://www.goodreads.com/quotes/619884-one-does-not-surrender-a-life-in-an-instant-that.

We find repentance difficult because it goes against all our sinful pride. We know that we should admit to our Father that we have done those things which ought not to be done and have left undone those things which ought to be done. But it makes us feel like we're a failure. And deep down we know we will probably do the same sin again, so that we fail even in our repentance. Then we don't want to go to our Father because we're ashamed of that failure. We are afraid he will look at us and reject us saying, "You are not my child." That is exactly what Satan wants us to think. Then the Spirit reminds us, "Rend your heart, and not your garments, and turn to the Lord your God: for he is gracious and merciful, slow to anger, and of great kindness, and repents of the evil" (Joel 2:12–13). So, when we do come, we will find open arms, tender fingers to wipe away tears, bleach to eradicate every sin, and forgiveness. We leave the throne with a skip in our step, freedom in our spirit, and an overflowing, merry love in our heart (2 Cor 7:11). When we grasp the fullness of joy that comes from knowing we are perfectly loved and reconciled with our Father through Christ, coveting fades away.

11

Conclusion

BY NOW IT IS obvious that the Ten Commandments overlap one another. In fact, each commandment encompasses all the others. Here is a summary of those implications.

1. If you have no other gods except God, then you won't make idols of anything else, will always keep his name holy, you'll obey his Sabbath, and commandments concerning authorities he established, concerning life, commitments, property, words, and heart attitudes.

2. To not make an idol of anything means not serving anything above God, not preferring our own words or those of the world when we speak of God, not serving our own pleasures on the Sabbath, not idolizing or disparaging authorities God installed, not placing our own will above God's in terms of life, vows, property, words, or wants.

3. To truly honor God's name means to love him from the heart above all else and to do what brings glory to him in worship, in priorities, in Sabbath observance, respect of authorities, life, promises, property, words, or even heart attitudes.

4. When we remember the Sabbath day, we are acknowledging God as Lord of our lives above all other competing gods, or

names, or authorities. We demonstrate to the world that life, peace, relationships, possessions, statements, and goals all have their consummation in something beyond this world.

5. Honoring and obeying parents and other authorities shows that we believe God to have established lower rulers and that we trust him to work through them. Therefore we don't idolize the servant authorities or what they represent; we don't misuse God's name by the way we live in submission to those authorities. We do submit to the jurisdiction of authorities, knowing that a day of perfect peace and justice is promised in the future. We respect contracts, people's property, and testimonies, without complaining. We worship God alone in contentment as our supreme authority.

6. If we don't murder, then we are affirming God's rule as God over all of life and creation. Nothing overpowers us to love it too much or to hate it, because God is our Lord. His name is revered as the source of all life. We rest (desist) from anger and hatred, willingly embrace authorities, don't diminish other's lives by desertion, theft, falsehood, or (even inwardly) through envy.

7. Because God is our husband, spiritual adultery occurs when we love and honor anything more than him. If we commit adultery, whether it is spiritual or physical, we say that our decisions and priorities are greater than God's, and we serve the idol of our own sinful heart. We dishonor God's name in us and do not rest in him as our completion, nor honor another's life; we diminish what belongs to our neighbor, falsely testify to our own glory, and are not content with our assignment in life.

8. To steal reveals again our choice to rebel against God's choices and idolize creation rather than the Creator. We steal God's glory and the glory of his name. We are not resting in his promised perfection and provision. We deny his authorities, diminish our neighbor's life and income, betray love and trust, lie about what is rightfully ours, and covet.

CONCLUSION

9. We have stopped reflecting God as truth, worshiping him alone, honoring his name, or believing that he honors truth, when we lie. A subterfuge of authorities is initiated. We murder our neighbor's reputation or his knowledge of truth, break expected oaths of truth, steal from other's storehouse of truth, and sometimes steal from other's labors, as when we cheat on a test. To inwardly covet means our hearts have been deceived as to what is truly important according to God's word.

10. Coveting is idolatrous, denying God as perfect Lord, dishonoring him, not waiting for his completion, rejecting the decisions of his authorities, being dismissive of other's lives or needs, belittling sacrificial covenants. It is the seed of theft, and merely pretends contentment.

My beautiful, perfect babies for whom I prayed before they even had two cells to their name were sinners. It hurt me, every time I saw sin in them, every time they fell short of the glory of God. These could not be my children, not the ones bathed in prayer and suckled with Scripture. They will never know their mother's wrenching pain over each rebellious rejection, the tears of torment over their souls. How could they? Their sinful hearts only knew their own deceit, which excused their actions.

I should not have been surprised at their sinfulness. God says all have sinned (Rom 3:23). I have sinned, we all have sinned and broken God's law. "If we say we have no sin, then the truth is not in us" (1 John 1:8). When I was a missionary, one of the local men told me that he had never sinned. He was a liar. Several years ago, God gave me an idea to make a chain of ten links out of different sized and colored pipe cleaners. Holding it up in front of my Sunday school kids, I asked, "If I undo this big, circular link, will the chain be broken?" Everyone's head nodded a "yes." "If I undo this little link, will the chain be broken?" Again, heads nodded yes. "Then it doesn't matter which commandment I break or how I break it, the chain of the law is still broken. I am a lawbreaker."

We think that it's okay to commit a "small" sin, at least small in our own estimation. I read once about a father whose children asked if they could see a movie with just a little immorality in it. He told them they could, if they would eat his brownies. They eagerly agreed. As he set the platter before them, he briefly commented that he had used good ingredients, but added just a little dog poop to the recipe. The children got the message, refraining from both the brownies and the movie.

In my Sunday school class, I have taken a pitcher and two glasses of water, one with many spoonfuls of dirt added, one with a grain of dirt. "Which glass can be added to the clear pitcher without making it impure?" Neither. In the same way, it doesn't matter if we sinned a little or a lot, we cannot come into the pure presence of a holy God.

Or we might excuse ourselves by saying we never broke any of God's commands. A young, unsaved, teenage boy in my car pool told me he had not sinned. I found myself explaining that sin was not just what we do, but included our thoughts and the whole attitude of our heart that was in rebellion against God. Had he always loved God with all his heart, mind, soul, and strength? If not, then he had broken the greatest commandment.

My sons were lawbreakers. They did not act like "my" sons. I could look at each and surmise, "That's not my child." But I was a lawbreaker. I did not act like God's child. If I were ashamed of my boys sometimes, how much more must God be ashamed and even angry with me. After all he had done in making me, providing for me, coming in human flesh to die for me, I had despised him. I had done this not only as a non-believer, but even more so as a believer, after I had tasted his grace! Yet God continued to love me. My sin was punished, as all sin must be. Either it falls on the perpetrator or a substitute, either on us or on Christ. But even if the ultimate death blow falls on Jesus rather than the saved Christian, there are still individual repercussions. That is why death comes to all. Without sin, there would be no death. All have sinned.

There is no way I can remove either the few or the many stains of my guilt. It is impossible to "clean myself up" before coming to

Conclusion

God. As I asked my young sons, "Is there any soap strong enough to wash away your sin? No? So what can wash away my sin? Nothing but the blood of Jesus." I have to come to him for that. I can't even use my own blood. Nothing else suffices.

But I not only need to be forgiven, I need to be made new from the innermost essence of me. I was born with a heart that hated God, but I also hardened my own heart. The Bible says that Pharaoh hardened his own heart, under God's sovereign will (Exod 7:3-4; 8:15; 9:39). It didn't happen because of his genes or his environment or some "irresistible" demonic force. He did it. I did it. We have all done it. God warns us not to harden our hearts like his people in the wilderness. Every sin rubs on our soul like a misshapen shoe causing a callus. I need a brand new heart, not just a little anti-bacterial handwash.

God promises that all those who come to him he will make his children. "But to all who did receive him, who believed in his name, he gave the right to become children of God, who were born, not of blood nor of the will of the flesh nor of the will of man, but of God" (John 1:12-13). God by his mercy gave me a new heart and made me his child.

Even though my children came out of my body, they don't necessarily act like my children. Even though God birthed me as his child, I don't always act like I am his. In fact, I never purely love him completely the way a true child should. When I first came to Jesus, in all my filthy rags, he gave me his Spirit, cleaned me up, gave me a new heart. But just like Peter at the Last Supper, I need to have my feet washed continually from the sin-laden dirt of the world that clings to me as I walk through this world.

God has promised to do this, too. "If we confess our sins, he is faithful and just to forgive us our sins, and to cleanse us from all unrighteousness" (1John 1:9). That doesn't mean just saying, "I'm sorry." We never taught our sons to say "sorry" because most of the time it would be a lie. We did expect them to say, "I have sinned. Please forgive me." I have not said this often enough to God. Daily confession keeps the soul soft, pliable, able to bend to God's will. But words without action are empty pitchers, promising a quenching of thirst, but delivering nothing. "Whoever says, 'I know him' but does not keep his commandments is a liar . . . whoever says he abides in him ought to walk in the same way in which he walked" (1 John 2:5–6).

Adam and Eve not only denied God as their Father when they disobeyed but also denied that they were children. Instead they proclaimed themselves to be their own, to belong to themselves alone. God later made the nation of Israel to be his children, his first-born. But Israel also failed to be his offspring. Each of us has gone astray, each of us has turned away. We all left the Garden of Eden in Adam. We all have been shut out from the tree of life in that garden. However, the wise woman told king David, "God does not take away life, but plans ways so that the banished one may not be cast out from him" (2 Sam 14:14). In a similar way, the Lord laid on Jesus the sin and punishment of our sin.

Jesus alone was God's true, obedient child, his only Son. He alone lived perfectly, loving his Father with all his heart, mind, soul and strength and his neighbor as himself. "Greater love has no one than this, that someone lays down his life for his friends." (John 15:13) There is one perfect child, only one. It is not you or I. We have only earned condemnation. But God has not treated us as our sins deserve. In Christ we are accepted in the beloved.

"There is therefore now no condemnation for those who are in Christ Jesus. For God has done what the law, weakened by the flesh, could not do. By sending his own Son in the likeness of sinful flesh and for sin, he condemned sin in the flesh, in order that the righteous requirement of the law might be fulfilled in us, who walk not according to the flesh but according to the Spirit" (Rom 8:1, 3–4).

He has fulfilled all requirements, all debts, all laws. Those who are hidden in him, who are in Christ through faith, have had God's pledge of adoption. Christ was the only child without sin. When the Father considered all his righteous laws, he could look at Jesus and say, "All others may have sinned, but not my Son." We have become his children, truly beloved children through Christ. Now we can in this life walk with him, obey him, depend on him, talk to him, make requests of him, and love God as our Father.

Conclusion

We can daily swim in the waters of everlasting grace, breathing in his loving life, empowered by his Spirit himself. All this is just a taste of what will come as those everlasting arms under us draw us closer into him, into an eternity of love. There we will rejoice and forever hear our Father tenderly call us, "My child."

Bibliography

Bunyan, John. *The Pilgrims Progress from This World to That Which Is to Come.* Cincinnati: Jennings and Graham, n.d.
Elliot, Elisabeth. "4 Elisabeth Elliot Quotes." http://www.goodreads.com/author/quotes/6264.Elisabeth_Elliot.
———. *Discipline: The Glad Surrender.* Old Tappan, NJ: F. H. Revell, 1982.
———. http://www.goodreads.com/quotes/355291-to-love-god-is-to-love-his-will-it-is.
———.http://www.goodreads.com/quotes/355292-jesus-loved-the-will-of-his-father-he-embraced-the.
———. http://www.goodreads.com/quotes/379879-the-willingness-to-be-and-to-have-just-what-god.
———. *Journals of Jim Elliot.* Grand Rapids, MI: Fleming H. Revell, 1978.
———. *The Liberty of Obedience: Some Thoughts on Christian Conduct and Service.* Waco, TX: Word, 1968.
———. *Passion and Purity: Learning to Bring Your Love Life under Christ's Control.* Grand Rapids, MI: Fleming H. Revell, 2002.
———. *Shadow of the Almighty: The Life and Testament of Jim Elliot.* Peabody, MA: Hendrickson, 2008.
———. *Taking Flight: Wisdom for Your Journey.* Grand Rapids: Baker, 2001.
———. *These Strange Ashes.* New York: Harper & Row, 1975.
Graham, Billy. *Decision* (July-August, 2011), 4.
Lewis, C. S. *The Weight of Glory.* Grand Rapids: Eerdmans, 1965.
Oecolampadius, Johannes. *In Isaiam Prophetum Hypomnematon, hoc est, commentariuorum, Ioannis Oecolammmmmmpadii Libri VI.* Basel: Cratander, 1525.
O'Neill, Eugene. http://www.brainyquote.com/citation/quotes/quotes/e/eugeneone163822.html?ct=Eugene+O%27Neill.
Poythress, Vern S. *The Shadow of Christ in the Law of Moses.* Brentwood, TN: Wolgemuth & Hyatt, 1991. Reprint. Phillipsburg, NJ: P & R, 1995.
Spurgeon, C. H. *Morning and Evening.* McLean, VA: MacDonald, n.d.
Taylor, Justin. "He Was No Fool." https://blogs.thegospelcoalition.org/justintaylor/2010/01/08/he-ws-no-fool/.
Tolkien, J. R. R. "On Fairy Stories." http://www.goodreads.com/quotes/6799505-i-would-venture-to-say-that-approaching-the-christian-story.

www.ingramcontent.com/pod-product-compliance
Lightning Source LLC
Chambersburg PA
CBHW071439160426
43195CB00013B/1966